Jewel Bowls

Jewel Boxes & Circular Lids

Jewel Box Necklace

Eyeglass Case

Round Zippered Pouches

CW01457633

Sugar Tree Ornament

Drawstring Bags

Chatelaines

Contents

1

Introduction

Who doesn't love hexies?

Paper Piecing is all the rage right now, and hexagons are still the most popular shape. But this doesn't mean that we are stuck making only Grandmother's Flower Garden! Adding a few other shapes to our hexagons can take hexies into the 21st century. The projects in this book combine hexagons and diamonds with half hexagons, equilateral triangles, squares, pentagons, and octagons to create some contemporary designs that are practical as well as beautiful.

About This Book

The projects in this book are small, using as few as 13 Paper Pieces! The largest project has only 52 Paper Pieces. Even if you have never paper pieced before, these projects will not be a huge commitment. Unlike many other sewing projects, paper piecing is mostly handwork and, therefore, very portable. It uses "found" time that may otherwise be wasted.

The projects in this book are each made using one of the following sizes of Paper Pieces: 1/2", 3/4", 1", 1-1/2" or 2". The number refers to the length of any one side of a Paper Piece. For example, each side of a 1" hexagon is exactly 1" in length. Each side of a 1" diamond is also 1" in length. This is also true for a triangle, square, pentagon, and octagon. So, any side of a 1" hexagon will fit perfectly to any side of a 1" diamond or any other 1" shape. **That is the magic of all the patterns in this book.**

Many of the items in this book can be made with several different sizes of Paper Pieces.

- 1" and larger Paper Pieces are much easier for a first project and work well with any quilting fabric.

- 3/4" Paper Pieces require a little more practice. It will be easier to work with the triangle and diamond shapes if the fabric chosen has a higher thread count that does not fray easily.

- 1/2" Paper Pieces require a little more skill. It is essential to choose a thinner fabric with a higher thread count such as a batik. Avoid fabrics that fray easily.

Projects in this book will often be described by the shape of the base, or bottom piece of the object. This will either be a triangle, square, pentagon, hexagon, or octagon.

General Instructions
English Paper Piecing Instructions

There are several English Paper Piecing techniques. This chapter will describe the two most common methods. Paper Pieces can be purchased from www.paperpieces.com and many local quilt shops.

Cutting and Basting

1) Cut your fabric. You may wish to pre-cut squares of fabric or conserve fabric by cutting pieces in rows. (Figs. 1 and 2)

Fig. 1

Pre-cut squares of fabric

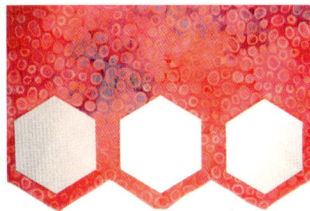 

Fig. 2

Conserve fabric by cutting pieces in rows

2) Pin the Paper Piece to the wrong side of the fabric. (Fig. 3)

3) Trim the fabric, leaving at least 1/4" seam allowance along all sides.

4) Fold the seam allowance over the edge of the Paper Piece, creating pleats at each corner. (Fig. 4)

5) Working from the back, baste one of two ways:

Basting through the paper and the fabric:

This method is recommended for beginners. It holds the fabric more securely to the Paper Piece and it eliminates most of the problems experienced by people just starting out. The basting stitches will need to be removed before the Paper Pieces can be removed.

Legend:

Paper Piece | Wrong Side of Fabric | Right Side of Fabric

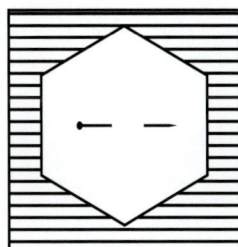

Fig. 3

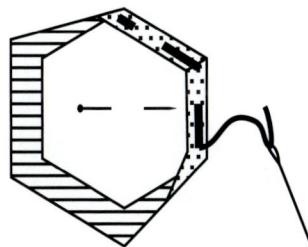

Fig. 4

Finished Piece

General Instructions

Basting through the fabric only:

This method is preferred by some experienced Paper Piecers. The basting stitches will not need to be removed later, leaving the raw edges on the back much neater. However, the fabric may shift during basting, and tiny Paper Pieces may be more difficult to remove later.

Legend:

Paper Piece   Wrong Side of Fabric   Right Side of Fabric

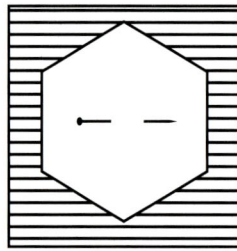

Fig. 3

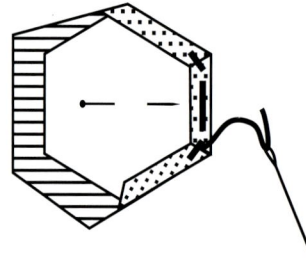

Fig. 4

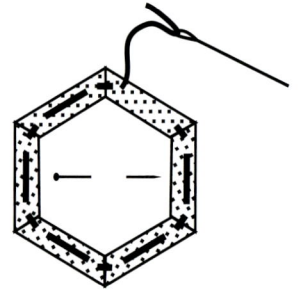

Finished Piece

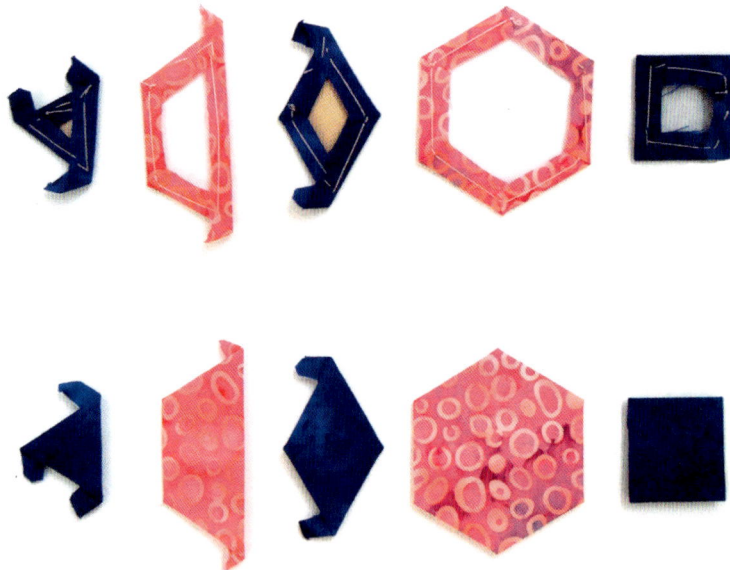

All photos in this book show basting though the fabric only.

When basting pointed shapes (diamonds, triangles and half hexies), let your "tails" wag. The "tails" can be tucked under the finished piece when joining it to the lining.

General Instructions

Joining Pieces

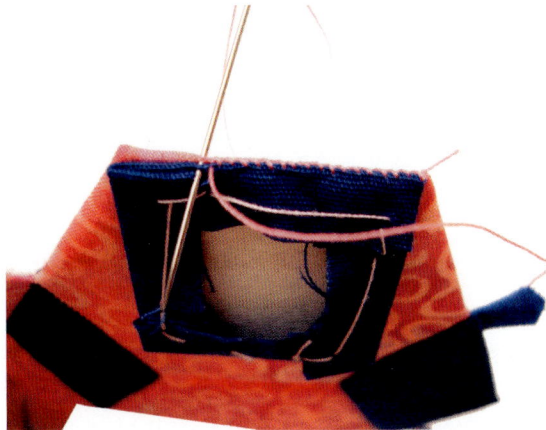

1) Place the right sides of the basted pieces together with the edges flush. Join the pieces with 8 -10 small whip stitches per inch. Remember to catch just the edges of the fabric.

2) Add an extra stitch at the beginning and end of each new side.

3) Secure with a knot. Bury the tail if desired.

• Paper Pieces are often easier to assemble as smaller units that are then joined together.

• It is not recommended that you remove any Paper Pieces until the piecing is finished and pressed. When instructed, take out the Paper Pieces. Remove the basting if you have sewn through the paper and the fabric. The Paper Pieces can be reused many times.

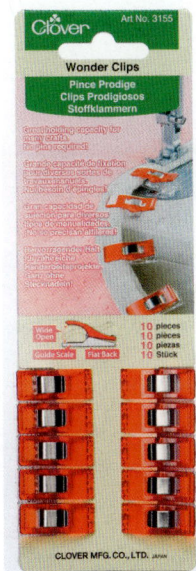

When joining pieces together, I find that using a clip or two to hold the items in place is very helpful. I highly recommend Clover Wonder Clips ®.

Fabric, Thread and Fusible

Fabric

One of the first things you should decide is which project you would like to create. The second decision should be which fabric to use. While you can use any fabric you like, I highly recommend a thin fabric with a high thread count such as a batik when making the smaller projects.

Most of the projects created in this book are made using two contrasting colors. A main color is chosen for the largest area that the hexagons and half hexagons create. A second contrasting color is chosen for the base, diamonds, and triangles. However, this is not the only way you can make them. Feel free to use as many fabrics as you like. Try making each section of diamonds a different color, or make all the hexagons a different color and keep the diamonds the same. The lining fabric can coordinate with the project or can add a nice surprise to the inside. Ever thought of making a change purse with the lining made out of fabric that has money printed on it? As you can see, the possibilities are endless! Just remember that, depending on how many fabrics you use, the fabric requirements will change slightly.

Thread

The thread you use is just as important as the fabric. If you are having trouble with your threads showing, try using a thinner thread for piecing and joining. Also, be sure you are not pulling too tightly or not tight enough. Just the right amount of tension will help you create a project without your stitches showing. Be sure you always match your thread to one of the colors of your fabric.

Fusible

Most of the projects in this book use 71F Pellon® Peltex® 1-Sided Fusible Ultra-Firm Stabilizer which is easy to find at your local quilt and fabric shops. The drawstring bag is the only exception, as it is made with 987F Pellon® Fusible Fleece.

Jewel Bowls

The hardest part might be choosing which bowl to start with. The possibilities are endless, but don't be overwhelmed! Making bowls is addictive, so you will want to make more than just one.

Jewel Bowls

Materials

1/2" Square Bottom
Finished Size
1-1/4" x 1-1/4" x 1-1/4"
Paper Pieces Required
(4) 1/2" Hexagons (HEX050)
(4) 1/2" Half Hexagons (HHX050)
(4) 1/2" 6 Point Diamonds (6DIA050)
(1) 1/2" Square (SQU050)

Fabric Required
Hexagons and Half Hexagons:
1-1/2" x 10"

Diamonds and Square:
1" x 7"

Lining:
2-1/2" x 5"

71F Pellon® Peltex® 1-Sided
Fusible Ultra-Firm
Stabilizer:
2" x 4-1/2"

3/4" Square Bottom
Finished Size
2" x 2" x 2"
Paper Pieces Required
(4) 3/4" Hexagons (HEX075)
(4) 3/4" Half Hexagons (HHX075)
(4) 3/4" 6 Point Diamonds (6DIA075)
(1) 3/4" Square (SQU075)

Fabric Required
Hexagons and Half Hexagons:
2" x 11"

Diamonds and Square:
1-1/4" x 8-1/4"

Lining:
3-1/4" x 7"

71F Pellon® Peltex® 1-Sided
Fusible Ultra-Firm
Stabilizer:
2-3/4" x 6-1/2"

1" Square Bottom
Finished Size
3" x 3" x 2-1/2"
Paper Pieces Required
(4) 1" Hexagons (HEX100)
(4) 1" Half Hexagons (HHX100)
(4) 1" 6 Point Diamonds (6DIA100)
(1) 1" Square (SQU100)

Fabric Required
Hexagons and Half Hexagons:
2-1/2" x 15"

Diamonds and Square:
1-1/2" x 10-1/2"

Lining:
4-1/4" x 9"

71F Pellon® Peltex® 1-Sided
Fusible Ultra-Firm
Stabilizer:
3-3/4" x 8-1/2"

1) Baste all Paper Pieces according to the general English Paper Piecing instructions on page 3.

2) Sew a half hexagon to the top of a hexagon. (Fig. 1)

3) Sew a diamond to the left side of the unit in Fig. 1. (Fig. 2)

Fig. 1
Make 4

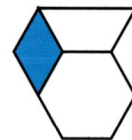

Fig. 2
Make 4

4) Sew all the units made in Fig. 2 together to make a row. Sew the square to the bottom of the first unit. (Fig. 3)

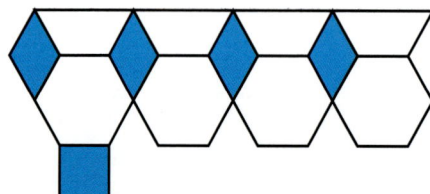

Fig. 3

5) Finish your bowl by following the directions on page 15.

Jewel Bowls

Materials

1/2" Pentagon Bottom
Finished Size
1-3/4" x 1-3/4" x 1-1/4"

Paper Pieces Required
(5) 1/2" Hexagons (HEX050)
(5) 1/2" Half Hexagons (HHX050)
(5) 1/2" 6 Point Diamonds (6DIA050)
(1) 1/2" Pentagon (PEN050)

Fabric Required
Hexagons and Half Hexagons:
1-1/2" x 12-1/2"

Diamonds and Pentagon:
1-1/2" x 6-1/4"

Lining:
2-3/4" x 6"

71F Pellon® Peltex® 1-Sided
Fusible Ultra-Firm
Stabilizer:
2-1/4" x 5-1/2"

3/4" Pentagon Bottom
Finished Size
2-3/4" x 2-3/4" x 1-3/4"

Paper Pieces Required
(5) 3/4" Hexagons (HEX075)
(5) 3/4" Half Hexagons (HHX075)
(5) 3/4" 6 Point Diamonds (6DIA075)
(1) 3/4" Pentagon (PEN075)

Fabric Required
Hexagons and Half Hexagons:
2" x 13-3/4"

Diamonds and Pentagon:
1-3/4" x 8"

Lining:
3-3/4" x 8-1/2"

71F Pellon® Peltex® 1-Sided
Fusible Ultra-Firm
Stabilizer:
3-1/4" x 8"

1" Pentagon Bottom
Finished Size
3-1/4" x 3-1/4" x 2-1/2"

Paper Pieces Required
(5) 1" Hexagons (HEX100)
(5) 1" Half Hexagons (HHX100)
(5) 1" 6 Point Diamonds (6DIA100)
(1) 1" Pentagon (PEN100)

Fabric Required
Hexagons and Half Hexagons:
2-1/2" x 18-3/4"

Diamonds and Pentagon:
2-1/4" x 9-1/2"

Lining:
4-3/4" x 11"

71F Pellon® Peltex® 1-Sided
Fusible Ultra-Firm
Stabilizer:
4-1/4" x 10-1/2"

1) Baste all Paper Pieces according to the general English Paper Piecing instructions on page 3.

2) Sew a half hexagon to the top of a hexagon. (Fig. 1)

3) Sew a diamond to the left side of the unit in Fig. 1. (Fig. 2)

Fig. 1
Make 5

Fig. 2
Make 5

4) Sew all the units made in Fig. 2 together to make a row. Sew the pentagon to the bottom of the first unit. (Fig. 3)

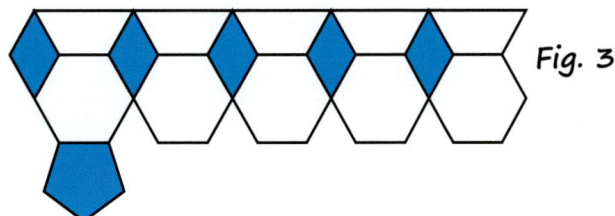

Fig. 3

5) Finish your bowl by following the directions on page 15.

Jewel Bowls

Materials

1/2" Hexagon Bottom
Finished Size
2" x 2" x 1-1/4"

Paper Pieces Required
(7) 1/2" Hexagons (HEX050)
(6) 1/2" Half Hexagons (HHX050)
(6) 1/2" 6 Point Diamonds (6DIA050)

Fabric Required
6 Hexagons and Half
Hexagons:
1-1/2" x 15"

Diamonds and 1 Hexagon:
1-1/2" x 7-1/2"

Lining:
3" x 7"

71F Pellon® Peltex® 1-Sided
Fusible Ultra-Firm
Stabilizer:
2-1/2" x 6-1/2"

3/4" Hexagon Bottom
Finished Size
3-1/4" x 3-1/4" x 1-3/4"

Paper Pieces Required
(7) 3/4" Hexagons (HEX075)
(6) 3/4" Half Hexagons (HHX075)
(6) 3/4" 6 Point Diamonds (6DIA075)

Fabric Required
6 Hexagons and Half
Hexagons:
2" x 16-1/2"

Diamonds and 1 Hexagon:
2" x 9"

Lining:
4" x 10"

71F Pellon® Peltex® 1-Sided
Fusible Ultra-Firm
Stabilizer:
3-1/2" x 9-1/2"

1" Hexagon Bottom
Finished Size
4" x 4" x 2-1/4"

Paper Pieces Required
(7) 1" Hexagons (HEX100)
(6) 1" Half Hexagons (HHX100)
(6) 1" 6 Point Diamonds (6DIA100)

Fabric Required
6 Hexagons and Half
Hexagons:
2-1/2" x 22-1/2"

Diamonds and 1 Hexagon:
2-1/4" x 11-1/2"

Lining:
5" x 13"

71F Pellon® Peltex® 1-Sided
Fusible Ultra-Firm
Stabilizer:
4-1/2" x 12-1/2"

1) Baste all Paper Pieces according to the general English Paper Piecing instructions on page 3.

2) Sew a half hexagon to the top of a hexagon. (Fig. 1)

3) Sew a diamond to the left side of the unit in Fig. 1. (Fig. 2)

Fig. 1
Make 6

Fig. 2
Make 6

4) Sew all the units made in Fig. 2 together to make a row. Sew the remaining hexagon to the bottom of the first unit. (Fig. 3)

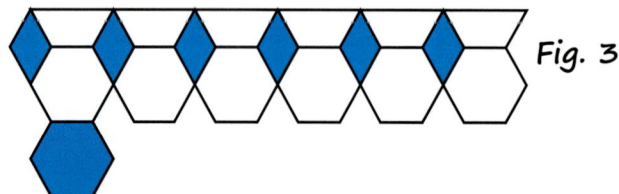

Fig. 3

5) Finish your bowl by following the directions on page 15.

Jewel Boxes

A jewel box is slightly deeper than the jewel bowl and can accommodate a lid. It's perfect for storing your accessories and can even be used as a small gift box.

Jewel Boxes

Materials

1/2" Square Bottom
Finished Size
1-1/4" x 1-1/4" x 1-3/4"

Paper Pieces Required
(8) 1/2" Hexagons (HEX050)
(4) 1/2" 6 Point Diamonds (6DIA050)
(4) 1/2" Equilateral Triangles (TRI050)
(1) 1/2" Square (SQU050)

Fabric Required
Hexagons:
1-1/2" x 12"

Diamonds, Triangles, and
Square:
1" x 7"

Lining:
3" x 5"

71F Pellon® Peltex® 1-Sided
Fusible Ultra-Firm
Stabilizer:
2-1/2" x 4-1/2"

3/4" Square Bottom
Finished Size
2" x 2" x 2-3/4"

Paper Pieces Required
(8) 3/4" Hexagons (HEX075)
(4) 3/4" 6 Point Diamonds (6DIA075)
(4) 3/4" Equilateral Triangles (TRI075)
(1) 3/4" Square (SQU075)

Fabric Required
Hexagons:
2" x 12"

Diamonds, Triangles, and
Square:
2-1/4" x 13-1/4"

Lining:
4" x 7"

71F Pellon® Peltex® 1-Sided
Fusible Ultra-Firm
Stabilizer:
3-1/2" x 6-1/2"

1" Square Bottom
Finished Size
3" x 3" x 3-1/2"

Paper Pieces Required
(8) 1" Hexagons (HEX100)
(4) 1" 6 Point Diamonds (6DIA100)
(4) 1" Equilateral Triangles (TRI100)
(1) 1" Square (SQU100)

Fabric Required
Hexagons:
2-1/2" x 18"

Diamonds, Triangles, and
Square:
1-1/2" x 17-1/2"

Lining:
5" x 9"

71F Pellon® Peltex® 1-Sided
Fusible Ultra-Firm
Stabilizer:
4-1/2" x 8-1/2"

1) Baste all Paper Pieces according to the general English Paper Piecing instructions on page 3.

2) Sew a hexagon to the top of a hexagon. (Fig. 1)

3) Sew a triangle and a diamond to the left side of the unit in Fig. 1. (Fig. 2)

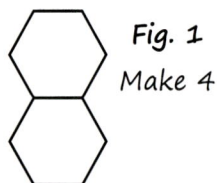

Fig. 1
Make 4

Fig. 2
Make 4

4) Sew all the units made in Fig. 2 together to make a row. Sew the square to the bottom of the first unit. (Fig. 3)

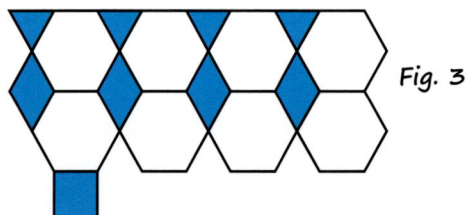

Fig. 3

5) Finish your box by following the directions on page 15.

Jewel Boxes

Materials

1/2" Pentagon Bottom
Finished Size
1-3/4" x 1-3/4" x 1-3/4"

Paper Pieces Required
(10) 1/2" Hexagons (HEX050)
(5) 1/2" 6 Point Diamonds (6DIA050)
(5) 1/2" Equilateral Triangles (TRI050)
(1) 1/2" Pentagons (PEN050)

Fabric Required

Hexagons:
1-1/2" x 15"

Diamonds, Triangles, and
Pentagon:
1-1/4" x 14"

Lining:
3-1/4" x 6"

71F Pellon® Peltex® 1-Sided
Fusible Ultra-Firm
Stabilizer:
2-3/4" x 5-1/2"

3/4" Pentagon Bottom
Finished Size
2-3/4" x 2-3/4" x 2-1/2"

Paper Pieces Required
(10) 3/4" Hexagons (HEX075)
(5) 3/4" 6 Point Diamonds (6DIA075)
(5) 3/4" Equilateral Triangles (TRI075)
(1) 3/4" Pentagon (PEN075)

Fabric Required

Hexagons:
2" x 15"

Diamonds, Triangles, and
Pentagon:
1-3/4" x 11-3/4"

Lining:
4-1/2" x 8-1/2"

71F Pellon® Peltex® 1-Sided
Fusible Ultra-Firm
Stabilizer:
4" x 8"

1" Pentagon Bottom
Finished Size
3-1/4" x 3-1/4" x 3-1/4"

Paper Pieces Required
(10) 1" Hexagons (HEX100)
(5) 1" 6 Point Diamonds (6DIA100)
(5) 1" Equilateral Triangles (TRI100)
(1) 1" Pentagon (PEN100)

Fabric Required

Hexagons:
2-1/2" x 22-1/2"

Diamonds, Triangles, and
Pentagon:
2-1/4" x 21"

Lining:
5-1/2" x 11"

71F Pellon® Peltex® 1-Sided
Fusible Ultra-Firm
Stabilizer:
5" x 10-1/2"

---

1) Baste all Paper Pieces according to the general English Paper Piecing instructions on page 3.

2) Sew a hexagon to the top of a hexagon. (Fig. 1)

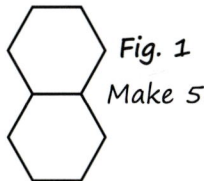

Fig. 1
Make 5

3) Sew a triangle and a diamond to the left side of the unit in Fig. 1. (Fig. 2)

Fig. 2
Make 5

4) Sew all the units made in Fig. 2 together to make a row. Sew the pentagon to the bottom of the first unit. (Fig. 3)

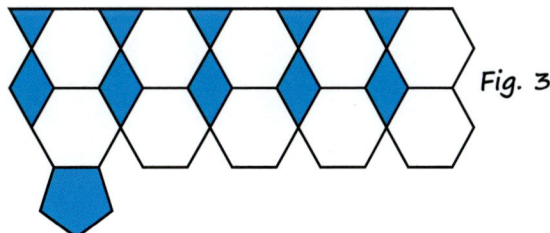

Fig. 3

5) Finish your box by following the directions on page 15.

Jewel Boxes

Materials

1/2" Hexagon Bottom
Finished Size
2" x 2" x 1-3/4"

Paper Pieces Required

(13) 1/2" Hexagons (HEX050)
(6) 1/2" 6 Point Diamonds (6DIA050)
(6) 1/2" Equilateral Triangles (TRI050)

Fabric Required

12 Hexagons:
1-1/2" x 18"

Diamonds, Triangles, and
1 Hexagon:
1-1/2" x 13-1/2"

Lining:
3-1/4" x 7"

71F Pellon® Peltex® 1-Sided
Fusible Ultra-Firm
Stabilizer:
2-3/4" x 6-1/2"

3/4" Hexagon Bottom
Finished Size
3-1/4" x 3-1/4" x 2-1/2"

Paper Pieces Required

(13) 3/4" Hexagons (HEX075)
(6) 3/4" 6 Point Diamonds (6DIA075)
(6) 3/4" Equilateral Triangles (TRI075)

Fabric Required

12 Hexagons:
2" x 18"

Diamonds, Triangles, and
1 Hexagon:
2" x 20"

Lining:
4-1/2" x 10"

71F Pellon® Peltex® 1-Sided
Fusible Ultra-Firm
Stabilizer:
4" x 9-1/2"

1" Hexagon Bottom
Finished Size
4" x 4" x 3-1/4"

Paper Pieces Required

(13) 1" Hexagons (HEX100)
(6) 1" 6 Point Diamonds (6DIA100)
(6) 1" Equilateral Triangles (TRI100)

Fabric Required

12 Hexagons :
2-1/2"x 27"

Diamonds, Triangles and
1 Hexagon:
2-1/4" x 20-1/2"

Lining:
5-3/4" x 13"

71F Pellon® Peltex® 1-Sided
Fusible Ultra-Firm
Stabilizer:
5-1/4" x 12-1/2"

1) Baste all Paper Pieces according to the general English Paper Piecing instructions on page 3.

2) Sew a hexagon to the top of a hexagon. (Fig. 1)

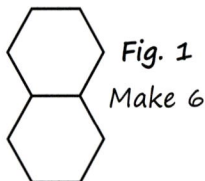

Fig. 1
Make 6

3) Sew a triangle and a diamond to the left side of the unit in Fig. 1. (Fig. 2)

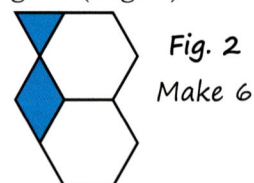

Fig. 2
Make 6

4) Sew all the units made in Fig. 2 together to make a row. Sew the remaining hexagon to the bottom of the first unit. (Fig. 3)

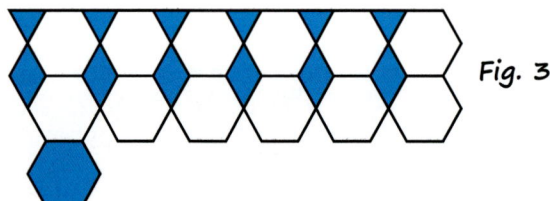

Fig. 3

5) Finish your box by following the directions on page 15.

Finishing Jewel Bowls and Boxes

Making the Lining

6) Press the finished piece with the Paper Pieces still in place. Be sure that all the edges are as straight and even as possible.

7) Lay the finished piece face up over the non-shiny side of the fusible, and trace with a marking tool. (Fig. 4)

Fig. 4

9) Lay the finished piece back over the fusible and flip the base piece back. With a marking tool, draw a line on the fusible at the fold. (Fig. 6)

Fig. 6

8) Take the finished piece off and cut the fusible 1/16" inside of the marked line. (Fig. 5)

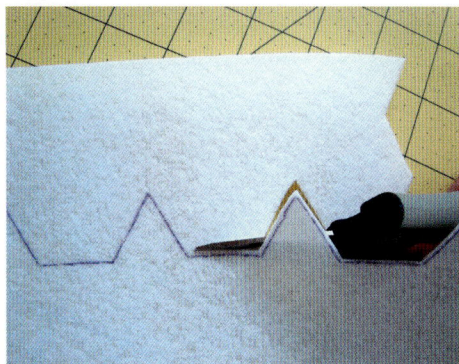

Fig. 5

10) Cut the fusible on the line. (Fig. 7)

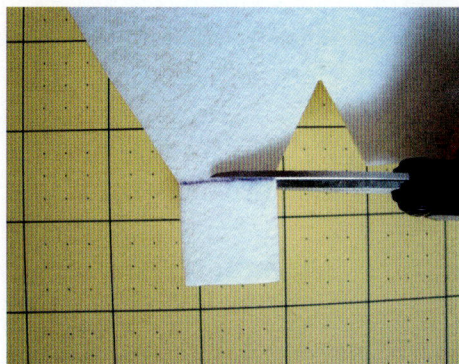

Fig. 7

11) Place the shiny side of the fusible down onto the wrong side of the lining fabric. Make sure to place the cut-off shape back in its original position.

12) Following the manufacturer's directions, iron the fusible to the back of the lining fabric.

13) Trim the lining fabric, leaving approximately 1/4" seam allowance on all sides. (Fig. 8)

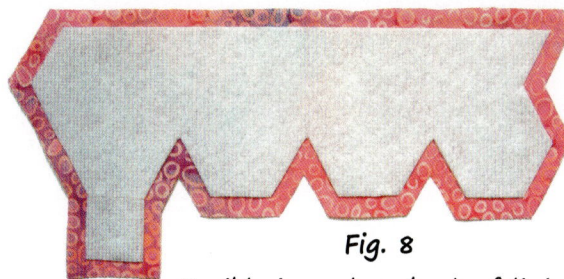

Fig. 8
Fusible ironed on back of lining

Finishing Jewel Bowls and Boxes

14) Clip the inside corners.

15) Fold the top straight edge of the lining over the fusible and press. (Fig. 9)

16) Fold the remaining seam allowances over the edges of the fusible creating pleats at each corner, and baste in place with thread. (Fig. 10)

Fig. 9

Fold straight edge over and press.

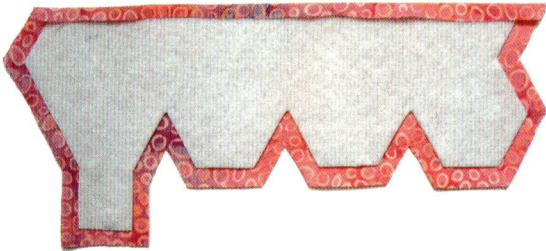

Fig. 10

Clip the inside corners and baste the seams down with thread.

17) Remove all Paper Pieces from the finished top.

18) *Optional*: If you are going to embellish your jewel bowl or box with crystals or beads, now is the time to attach them. It is much easier to add them now, while the piece is flat, than it will be when the bowl or box is completed. See embellishments section on page 55 for more information.

19) With wrong sides together, join the finished piece to the lining using a combination of blind and whip stitches. Stitches will be less visible with the blind stitch, but a whip stitch with a shorter stitch length will be necessary for the inner corners where the seam allowance on the lining is very narrow. (Figs. 11 and 12)

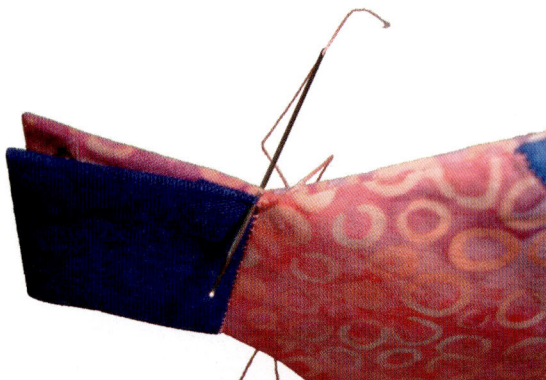

Fig. 11

Whip stitch for inner corner

Fig. 12

Blind stitched together

Finishing Jewel Bowls and Boxes

20) The diagrams below show the order in which the sides should be stitched together. Make sure the stitches are taut. A clip may be helpful to hold sections together while joining.

Jewel Bowl Joining Layouts

Square Bottom Bowl

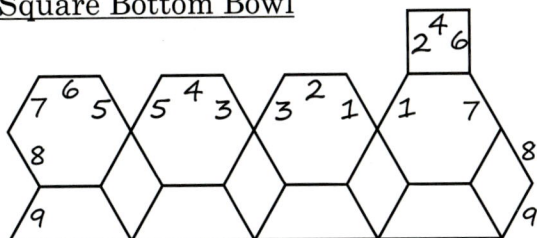

Pentagon Bottom Bowl

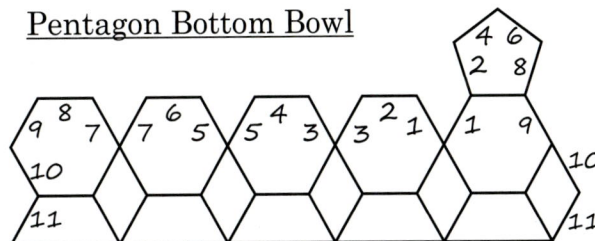

Hexagon Bottom Bowl

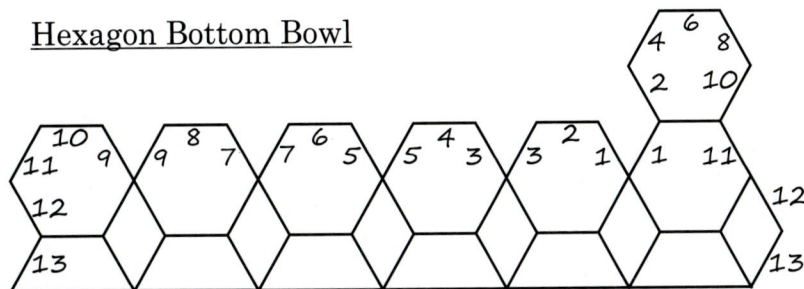

Jewel Box Joining Layouts

Square Bottom Box

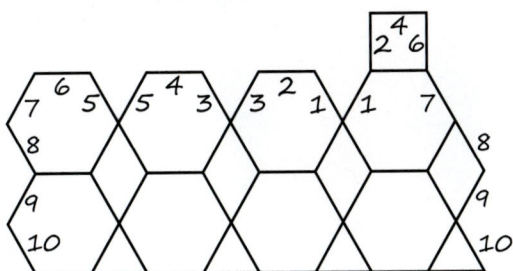

Pentagon Bottom Box

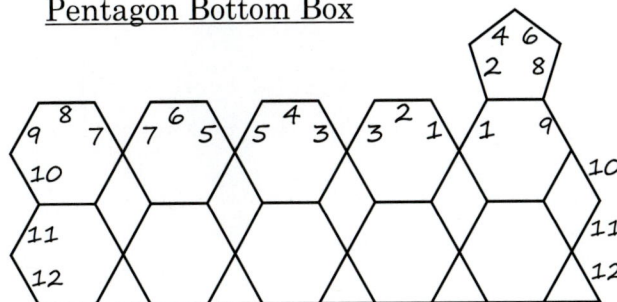

Hexagon Bottom Box

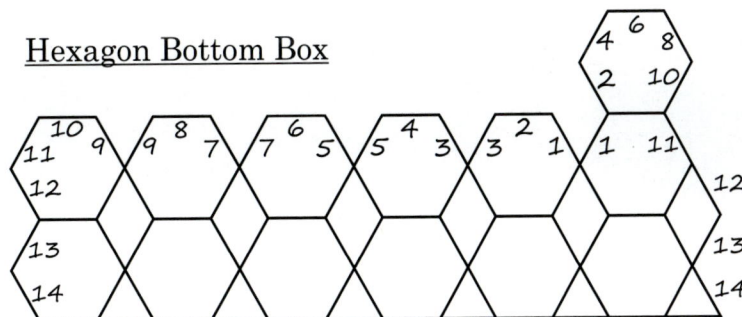

Finishing Jewel Bowls and Boxes

21) Working from the right side, assemble the jewel bowl or box. Join the shapes together with a closely spaced whip stitch through the top layer only. (Figs. 13 and 14)

22) After joining sides 1 and 2, travel the thread between the layers of fabric to the next starting point. Secure the thread with an extra stitch and repeat until all sides of the base unit are joined. (Fig. 15)

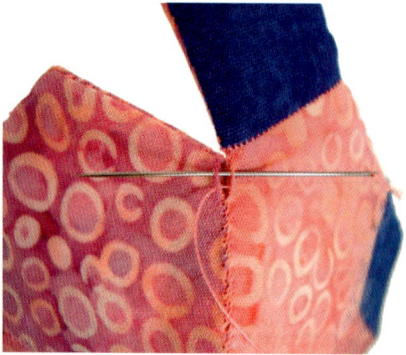

Fig. 13

Joining side 1

Fig. 14

Joining side 2

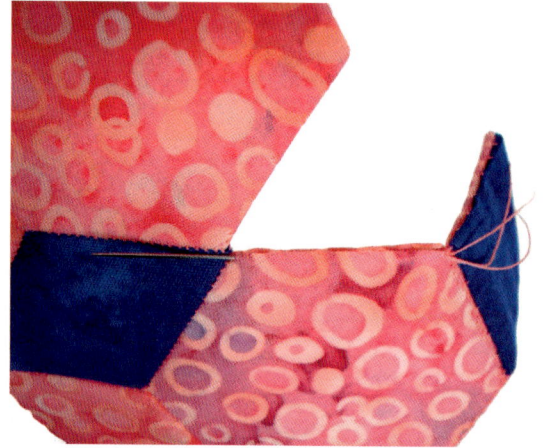

Fig. 15

Travel the thread to the start of the next side.

23) When the entire piece has been whip stitched together, secure the lining on the top edge with a few extra stitches. This will help keep the shape of the bowl or box.

Finished Jewel Bowl

Finished Jewel Box

24) If you are making the box, make the lid following the instructions on page 19.

Finished Jewel Box with Lid

Circular Box Lids

Materials

1/2" Square Bottom Box
- Lid -
Paper Pieces Required
(1) 1-1/2" Circle (CIRC150)
(1) 1/2" x 4-7/8" Rectangle (REC050x478)

Fabric Required
Circles and Rectangles:
4-3/4" x 5-3/4"

Lining:
4-3/4" x 5-3/4"

71F Pellon® Peltex® 1-Sided
Fusible Ultra-Firm Stabilizer:
2-3/4" x 5-1/4"

3/4" Square Bottom Box
- Lid -
Paper Pieces Required
(1) 2" Circle (CIRC200)
(1) 3/4" x 7" Rectangle (REC075x700)

Fabric Required
Circles and Rectangles:
5-3/4" x 7-3/4"

Lining:
5-3/4" x 7-3/4"

71F Pellon® Peltex® 1-Sided
Fusible Ultra-Firm Stabilizer:
3-3/4" x 7-1/4"

1" Square Bottom Box
- Lid -
Paper Pieces Required
(1) 2-3/4" Circle (CIRC275)
(1) 1" x 9" Rectangle (REC100x900)

Fabric Required
Circles and Rectangles:
6-3/4" x 9-3/4"

Lining:
6-3/4" x 9-3/4"

71F Pellon® Peltex® 1-Sided
Fusible Ultra-Firm Stabilizer:
4" x 9-1/4"

1/2" Pentagon Bottom Box
- Lid -
Paper Pieces Required
(1) 1-7/8" Circle (CIRC178)
(1) 1/2" x 6" Rectangle (REC050x600)

Fabric Required
Circles and Rectangles:
5" x 6-3/4"

Lining:
5" x 6-3/4"

71F Pellon® Peltex® 1-Sided
Fusible Ultra-Firm Stabilizer:
3" x 6-1/4"

3/4" Pentagon Bottom Box
- Lid -
Paper Pieces Required
(1) 2-3/4" Circle (CIRC275)
(1) 3/4" x 8-1/2" Rectangle (REC075x850)

Fabric Required
Circles and Rectangles:
6-1/4" x 9-1/4"

Lining:
6-1/4" x 9-1/4"

71F Pellon® Peltex® 1-Sided
Fusible Ultra-Firm Stabilizer:
3-3/4" x 8-3/4"

1" Pentagon Bottom Box
- Lid -
Paper Pieces Required
(1) 3-1/2" Circle (CIRC350)
(1) 1" x 11-1/4" Rectangle
(REC100x11025)

Fabric Required
Circles and Rectangles:
7-1/4" x 12"

Lining:
7-1/4" x 12"

71F Pellon® Peltex® 1-Sided
Fusible Ultra-Firm Stabilizer:
5-3/4" x 11-1/2"

1/2" Hexagon Bottom Box
- Lid -
Paper Pieces Required
(1) 2-1/4" Circle (CIRC225)
(1) 1/2" x 7-1/8" Rectangle (REC050x718)

Fabric Required
Circles and Rectangles:
5-1/2" x 8"

Lining:
5-1/2" x 8"

71F Pellon® Peltex® 1-Sided
Fusible Ultra-Firm Stabilizer:
3" x 7-1/2"

3/4" Hexagon Bottom Box
- Lid -
Paper Pieces Required
(1) 3-1/4" Circle (CIRC325)
(1) 3/4" x 10-1/4" Rectangle
(REC075x10025)

Fabric Required
Circles and Rectangles:
6-3/4" x 11"

Lining:
6-3/4" x 11"

71F Pellon® Peltex® 1-Sided
Fusible Ultra-Firm Stabilizer:
4-1/4" x 10-1/2"

1" Hexagon Bottom Box
- Lid -
Paper Pieces Required
(1) 4" Circle (CIRC400)
(1) 1" x 13" Rectangle
(REC100x1300)

Fabric Required
Circles and Rectangles:
6-3/4" x 13-3/4"

Lining:
6-3/4" x 13-3/4"

71F Pellon® Peltex® 1-Sided
Fusible Ultra-Firm Stabilizer:
5-1/4" x 13-1/4"

Circular Box Lids

Construction for Top of Lid

I like to use Karen Kay Buckley's Perfect Circles® technique for the circular lid. More information can be found on her website, www.KarenKayBuckley.com.

1) Place the Paper Piece circle or Perfect Circle ® on the non-shiny side of the fusible, and trace around it with a marking tool.

2) Cut just inside the traced line on the fusible to create a circle **exactly** the same size as the Paper Piece or Perfect Circle ®.

3) From the fabric, cut 2 circles with at least 1/4" seam allowance.

4) Place the shiny side of the fusible circle down onto the wrong side of the first fabric circle. Following the manufacturer's directions, iron the fusible to the back of the fabric circle.

5) Pin the Paper Piece circle, or place the Perfect Circle® on the wrong side of the second fabric circle.

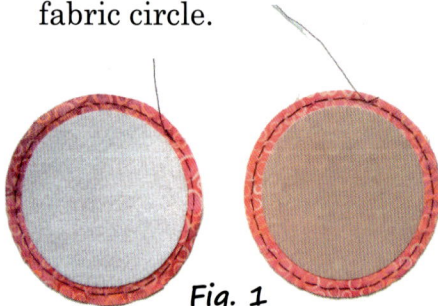

Fig. 1

Running stitch in seam allowance

Fig. 2

Gathered fabric around fusible circle and Paper Piece circle or Perfect Circle ®

6) With a needle and thread, sew a running stitch in the seam allowance all the way around each circle. (Fig. 1)

7) Gently pull the thread to gather the fabric around the circle with the Paper Piece or Perfect Circle ®. Do the same for the circle with the fusible. (Fig. 2)

8) Lightly apply spray starch to the gathered seam allowances of both circles and press until dry with a dry iron.

9) Remove the Paper Piece or Perfect Circle ®.

10) Place wrong sides together and slip stitch the two fabric circles together.

Construction for Sides of Lid

11) Place the Paper Piece rectangle on the non-shiny side of the fusible, and trace around it with a marking tool.

12) Cut just inside the traced line on the fusible to create a rectangle EXACTLY the same size as the Paper Piece rectangle.

Circular Box Lids

Fig. 3

Fusible rectangle and
Paper Piece rectangle with
seam allowance

Fig. 4

Basted fabric around
fusible rectangle and
Paper Piece rectangle

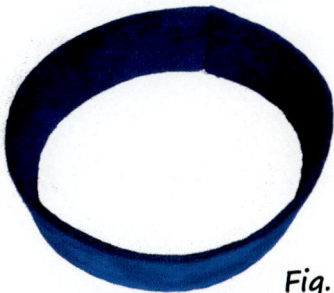

Fig. 5

Rectangle formed into a ring

13) From the fabric, cut 2 rectangles with at least 1/4" seam allowance. (Fig. 3)

14) Place the shiny side of the fusible down onto the wrong side of the fabric. Follow the manufacturer's directions and press it in place.

15) Pin the Paper Piece rectangle to the wrong side of the second fabric rectangle.

16) Baste the fabric in place on both rectangles. (Fig. 4)

17) Press and remove the Paper Piece.

18) With the wrong sides together, join the rectangles with a blind stitch.

19) Press again.

20) Whip stitch the ends of the rectangle together, forming a ring. Be sure the side with the fusible faces towards the inside of the lid. (Fig. 5)

21) Lay the circular top, fused-side-up, over the ring and tack with short appliqué pins. (Fig. 6)

22) Attach the circular top to the sides of the lid with a whip stitch. Be sure to pull your stitches taut.

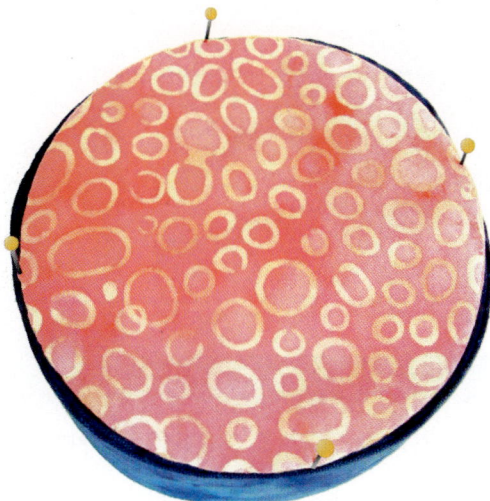

Fig. 6
Circular top attached with appliqué pins

Finished Circular Box Lid

Jewel Box Necklace

The Jewel Box Necklace is a great place to safely store your thimble or rings while doing activities that may put them in danger, such as washing dishes.

Jewel Box Necklace

Materials

1/2" Square Bottom
Finished Size
1-1/4" x 1-1/4" x 2"

Paper Pieces Required
(8) 1/2" Hexagons (HEX050)
(4) 1/2" 6 Point Diamonds (6DIA050)
(4) 1/2" Equilateral Triangles (TRI050)
(1) 1/2" Square (SQU050)
(1) 1-1/4" Square (SQU125)
(1) 1/2" x 5" Rectangle (REC050x500)

Fabric Required

Hexagons, 1-1/4" Square,
Rectangle, and Lining:
7-1/2" x 13"

Diamonds, Triangles, and
1/2" Square:
1" x 7"

71F Pellon® Peltex® 1-Sided
Fusible Ultra-Firm
Stabilizer:
5" x 5-1/2"

Items Required
Metal Chain:
31" or desired length

Optional Embellishments:
(29) hot-fix flat back crystals

Square Lid

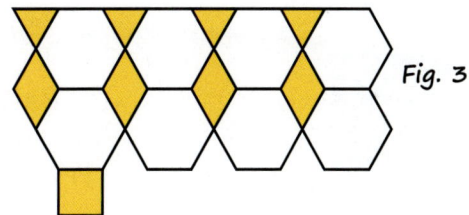

Fig. 4
Fusible square and rectangles

1) Baste all Paper Pieces according to the general English Paper Piecing instructions on page 3.

2) Sew a hexagon to the top of a hexagon. (Fig. 1)

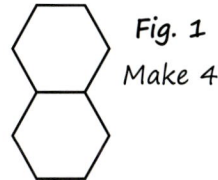

Fig. 1
Make 4

3) Sew a triangle and a diamond to the left side of the unit in Fig. 1. (Fig. 2)

Fig. 2
Make 4

4) Sew all the units made in Fig. 2 together to make a row. Sew the square to the bottom of the first unit. (Fig. 3)

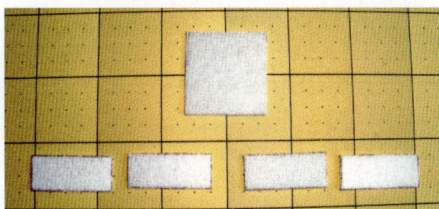

Fig. 3

5) Finish the bottom of the jewel box necklace by following the directions on page 15 and then continue to make the square box lid.

> The fusible makes the opening naturally round. Once it is finished, be sure to pinch the corners of the top edge to square up the bottom of the jewel box necklace.

6) Place the 1-1/4" square Paper Piece on the non-shiny side of the fusible and trace around it with a marking tool.

7) Cut just inside the traced line on the fusible to create a square **exactly** the same size as the Paper Piece square. (Fig. 4)

8) From the remaining fusible, cut four 1/2" x 1-1/4" rectangles. (Fig. 4)

Jewel Box Necklace

Fig. 5

Fusible fused on wrong side of fabric

Fig. 6

Basted fabric around fusible
and Paper Pieces

Fig. 7

Blind stitched square and rectangle

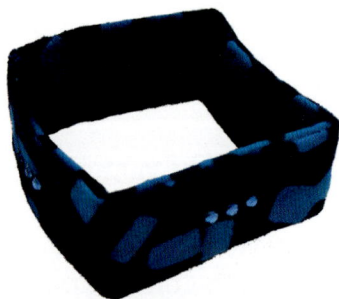

Fig. 8

Embellished and finished sides
of the lid

9) From the fabric, cut 2 squares and 2 rectangles with at least 1/4" seam allowance using the Paper Pieces as a guide.

10) Place the four fusible rectangles end-to-end and shiny-side-down on the wrong side of the first fabric rectangle.
   • Compare the length of the four fusible rectangles to the Paper Piece rectangle making sure they are **exactly** the same size.
   • Either move the fusible rectangles closer, or trim them slightly to make sure they are the same length.
   • Follow the manufacturer's directions and press them in place. (Fig. 5)

11) Place the shiny side of the fusible square down onto the wrong side of the fabric. Follow the manufacturer's directions and press it in place. (Fig. 5)

12) Pin the Paper Piece rectangle to the wrong side of the second fabric rectangle. Do the same for the Paper Piece square.

13) Baste the fabric in place on all pieces. (Fig. 6)

14) Press and remove Paper Pieces.

15) With the wrong sides together, join the rectangles with a blind stitch. Do the same for the squares. (Fig. 7)

16) Press again.

17) *Optional:* If you are going to embellish your lid top and/or sides with crystals or beads, now is the time to attach them. It is much easier to add them now, while the piece is flat, than it will be when the necklace is completed. Be sure to add them to the **fused-side up** on the square and the **fused-side down** on the rectangle. See embellishments section on page 55 for more information.

Jewel Box Necklace

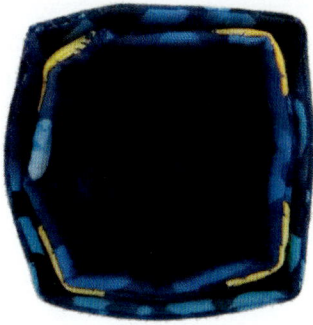

Fig. 9
Checking to make sure
sides of the lid fit the
finished jewel box bottom

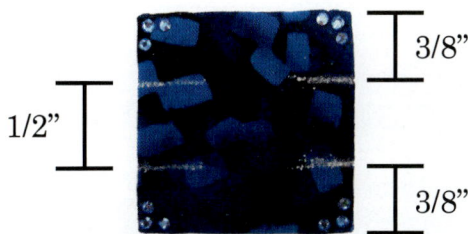

1/2"
3/8"
3/8"

Fig. 10
Square top marked with
1/2" gaps

Fig. 11
Square top attached to sides of
the lid with pins.

Be sure to leave the spaces
between the marks unstitched.

18) With the fusible on the **inside**, join the ends of the rectangle, forming a square. Check and make sure it will slide over the edge of your finished jewel box. (Figs. 8 and 9)

19) With the **fused-side up**, use an erasable marker to mark 3/8" from the bottom and top edges on opposite sides of the square. (Fig. 10)

20) With the **fused-side up**, place the marked square over the sides of the lid and tack with short appliqué pins. (Fig. 11)

21) Attach the top to the sides of the lid using a whip stitch. Be sure to leave the spaces between the marks unstitched for the chain to pass through.

22) Cut the chain to the desired length.

23) Using a strong thread, attach one end of the chain securely to the top edge of the finished jewel box.

24) Run the chain up inside the lid, through the unstitched gap, and back down through the gap on the opposite side of the lid.

25) Using a strong thread, attach the end of the chain securely to the top edge of the finished jewel box. (Fig. 12)

Fig. 12
Lid attached to the box by the chain going
through the gaps in the lid

Eyeglass Case

This stylish eyeglass case is the perfect place to store your favorite pair of shades. Don't be surprised if your friends ask you to make one for them!

Eyeglass Case

Materials

1) Baste all Paper Pieces according to the general English Paper Piecing instructions on page 3.

2) For **each** of the five coordinating fabrics, join 3 hexagons in a column with a half hexagon on the top. Join the remaining hexagon to the remaining half hexagon. (Fig. 1)

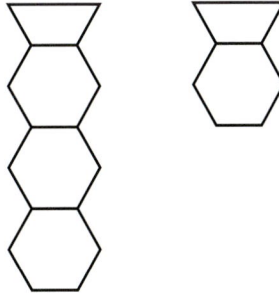

Fig. 1
Make 5 of each column

3) Sew the diamonds to the left side of the columns made in Fig. 1. (Fig. 2)

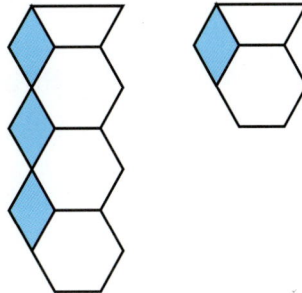

Fig. 2
Make 5 of each column

4) Sew the columns made in Fig. 2 together to create the body and cap of the case. (Fig. 3) Be sure to watch the fabric placement. The body and the cap should be a mirror image of each other.

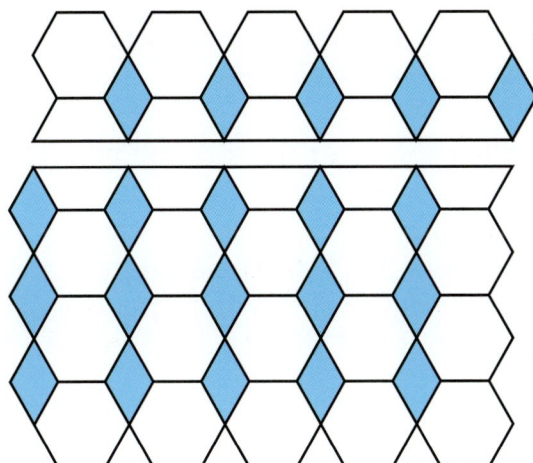

Cap of case

Fig. 3

Body of case

Eyeglass Case

Fig. 4

Making the Lining

Fig. 5

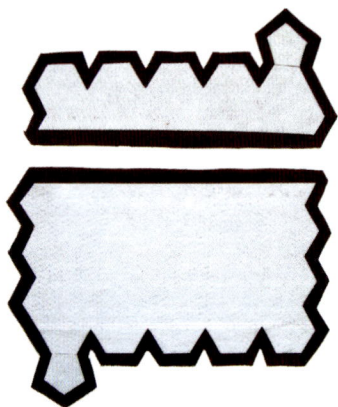

Fig. 6

Fig. 7

5) Sew a pentagon to the bottom of the hexagon on the end of the first unit on the case body. Do the same for the case cap. (Fig. 4)

6) Press both pieces with the papers still in them. Be sure that all the edges are as straight and even as possible.

7) Lay the finished piece for the case body face up over the non-shiny side of the fusible and trace with a marking tool.

8) Cut the fusible 1/16" inside of the marked line **except** for the straight edge.

9) Lay the finished piece back over the fusible and flip the pentagon back. With a marking tool, draw a line on the fusible at the fold. Cut the fusible on the line. (Fig. 5)

10) Repeat step 7 through 9 for the case cap.

11) Using a rotary cutter and a ruler, cut 1/8" off the straight edges of both pieces of the fusible. This will ensure that the lining does not interfere with the zipper.

12) Make the lining for the case body. Place the shiny side of the fusible down on the wrong side of the lining fabric. Make sure to place the fusible pentagon back in its original position.

13) Following the manufacturer's directions, iron the fusible to the back of the lining fabric.

14) Trim the lining fabric, leaving approximately 1/4" seam allowance on all sides. (Fig. 6)

15) Fold the seam allowance over the straight edge of the fusible and press.

16) Clip the inside corners. Fold the remaining seam allowances over the edge of the fusible, creating pleats at the corners. Baste all sides in place with thread. (Fig. 7)

17) Repeat steps 12 through 16 for the case cap.

18) Remove all Paper Pieces.

Eyeglass Case

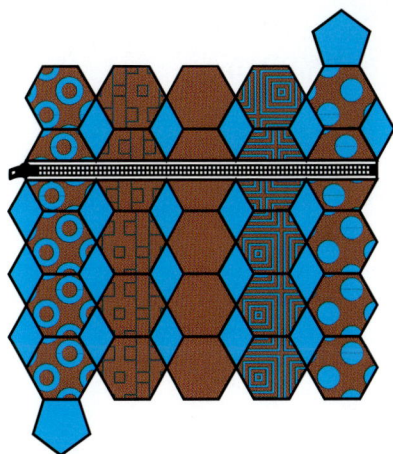

Fig. 8

Make sure you pin the zipper so the pull is on the outside of the case.

Fig. 9

19) Lay the straight edge of the case body and cap on either side of the zipper. Determine the exact length needed for the zipper and shorten the zipper if necessary.

20) Pin the zipper in place, tucking the ends under. Be sure to match up the patterns on either side of the zipper. (Fig. 8)

21) Use the zipper foot attachment on your sewing machine to top stitch the zipper in place.

Match the bobbin thread to the color of your zipper as the thread will show on the inside of the case.

22) Flip the finished piece over. With the wrong sides together, pin the basted lining for the cap to the finished case cap.

23) Join the finished piece to the lining using a combination of blind and whip stitches. Stitches will be less visible with the blind stitch, but a whip stitch with a shorter stitch length will be necessary for the inner corners where the seam allowance on the lining is very narrow. Sew the irregular sides **first**, saving the straight edge for **last**. (Fig. 9)

24) Repeat steps 22 and 23 for the case body. This will finish the lining for the case.

25) The diagrams below show the order in which the sides should be stitched together. Make sure the stitches are taut. A clip may be helpful to hold sections together while joining.

Case Cap

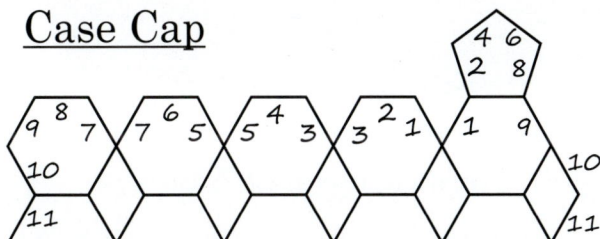

Case Body

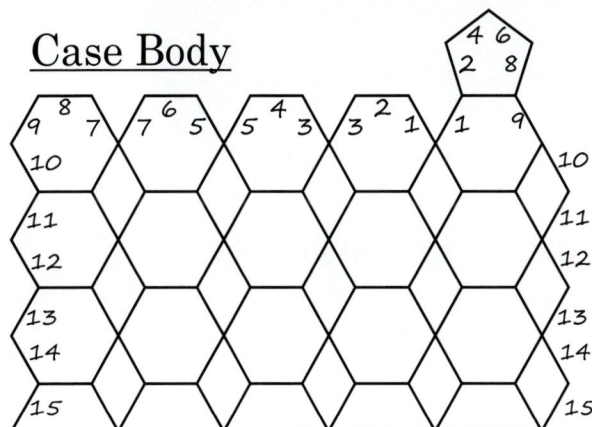

Eyeglass Case

26) Working from the right side, assemble the cap for the case. Join the shapes together with a closely spaced whip stitch through the top layer only. (Fig. 10)

27) After joining sides 1 and 2, travel the thread between the layers of fabric to the next starting point. Secure the thread with an extra stitch and repeat until all sides of the cap unit are joined. (Fig. 11)

28) Repeat steps 26 and 27 for the case body.

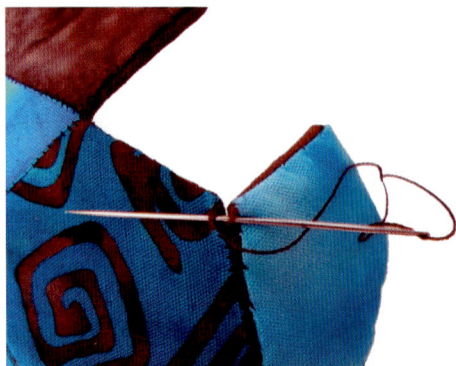

Fig. 10
Joining side 2

Fig. 11
Travel the thread to the start of the next side.

Case cap completed

Finished Eyeglass Case

Round Zippered Pouches

Need a new makeup bag? How about a coin purse? The Round Zippered Pouch is the perfect place to keep those odds and ends.

Round Zippered Pouches

Materials

1/2" Small Round Zippered Pouch
Finished Size
2-1/2" x 2-1/2" x 2-1/2"

Paper Pieces Required
(14) 1/2" Hexagons (HEX050)
(12) 1/2" Half Hexagons (HHX050)
(12) 1/2" 6 Point Diamonds (6DIA050)

Fabric Required
12 Hexagons and
12 Half Hexagons:
1-1/2" x 33"

Diamonds and 2 Hexagons:
1-1/2" x 12"

Lining:
5-1/2" x 7"

71F Pellon® Peltex® 1-Sided
Fusible Ultra-Firm
Stabilizer:
4" x 6-1/2"

Items Required
Zipper:
7"

3/4" Medium Round Zippered Pouch
Finished Size
3-1/2" x 3-1/2" x 3-1/2"

Paper Pieces Required
(14) 3/4" Hexagons (HEX075)
(12) 3/4" Half Hexagons (HHX075)
(12) 3/4" 6 Point Diamonds (6DIA075)

Fabric Required
12 Hexagons and
12 Half Hexagons:
2" x 36"

Diamonds and 2 Hexagons:
1-3/4" x 15"

Lining:
7" x 10"

71F Pellon® Peltex® 1-Sided
Fusible Ultra-Firm
Stabilizer:
5-3/4" x 9"

Items Required
Zipper:
9"

1" Large Round Zippered Pouch
Finished Size
4-1/2" x 4-1/2" x 4-1/2"

Paper Pieces Required
(14) 1" Hexagons (HEX100)
(12) 1" Half Hexagons (HHX100)
(12) 1" 6 Point Diamonds (6DIA100)

Fabric Required
12 Hexagons and
12 Half Hexagons:
2-1/2" x 49-1/2"

Diamonds and 2 Hexagons:
2-1/4" x 18"

Lining:
8-3/4" x 13"

71F Pellon® Peltex® 1-Sided
Fusible Ultra-Firm
Stabilizer:
7-1/2" x 12-1/2"

Items Required
Zipper:
12"

1) Baste all Paper Pieces according to the general English Paper Piecing instructions on page 3.

2) Sew a half hexagon to the top of a hexagon made from the same fabric. (Fig. 1)

3) Sew a diamond to the left side of the unit in Fig. 1. (Fig. 2)

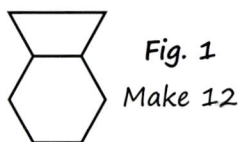

Fig. 1
Make 12

Fig. 2
Make 12

4) Sew 6 of the units made in Fig. 2 together to make a row. Sew the remaining hexagon to the bottom of the first unit. (Fig. 3)

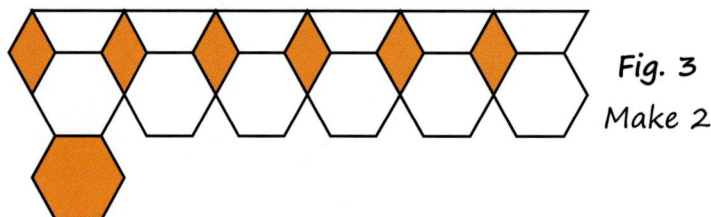

Fig. 3
Make 2

Round Zippered Pouches

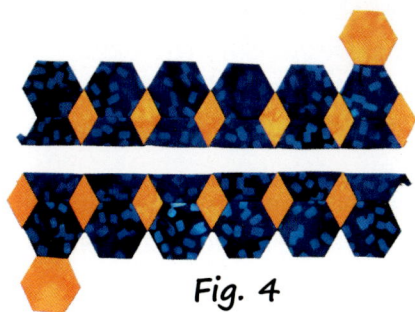
Fig. 4

Making the Lining

Fig. 5

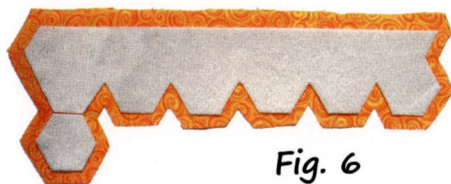
Fig. 6

Fig. 7

5) Press both finished pieces with the Paper Pieces still in place. Be sure that all the edges are as straight and even as possible. (Fig. 4)

6) Lay one of the finished pieces face up over the non-shiny side of the fusible and trace with a marking tool.

7) Cut the fusible 1/16" inside of the marked line **except** for the straight edge.

8) Lay the finished piece back over the fusible and flip the base hexagon back. With a marking tool, draw a line on the fusible at the fold. Cut the fusible on the line. (Fig. 5)

9) Repeat steps 6 through 8 for the other half.

10) Using a rotary cutter and a ruler, cut 1/8" off the straight edges of both pieces of the fusible. This will ensure that the lining does not interfere with the zipper.

11) Make the lining for one half of the pouch. Place the shiny side of the fusible down on the wrong side of the lining fabric. Make sure to place the fusible pentagon back in its original position.

12) Following the manufacturer's directions, iron the fusible to the back of the lining fabric.

13) Trim the lining fabric, leaving approximately 1/4" seam allowance on all of the sides. (Fig. 6)

14) Fold the seam allowance over the straight edge of the fusible and press.

15) Clip the inside corners. Fold the remaining seam allowances over the edges of the fusible, creating pleats at the corners. Baste all sides in place with thread. (Fig. 7)

16) Repeat steps 11 through 15 for the other half of the pouch.

17) Remove all Paper Pieces.

Round Zippered Pouches

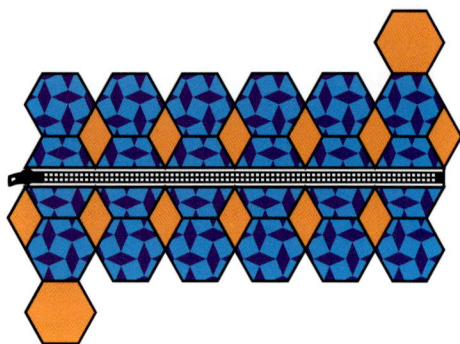

Fig. 8

Make sure you pin the zipper so the pull is on the outside of the case.

18) Lay the straight edge of the pieced halves on either side of the zipper. Determine the exact length needed for the zipper, and shorten the zipper if necessary.

19) Pin the zipper in place, tucking the ends under. Be sure to match up the patterns on either side of the zipper. (Fig. 8)

20) Use the zipper foot attachment on your sewing machine to top stitch the zipper in place.

Match the bobbin thread to the color of your zipper as the thread will show on the inside of the case.

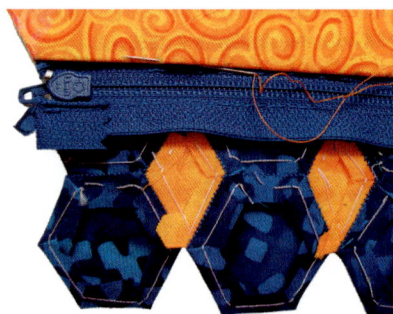

Fig. 9

Fig. 10

21) Flip the finished piece over. With the wrong sides together, pin the basted lining to one half of the finished pouch.

22) Join the finished piece to the lining using a combination of blind and whip stitches. Stitches will be less visible with the blind stitch, but a whip stitch with a shorter stitch length will be necessary for the inner corners where the seam allowance on the lining is very narrow. Sew the irregular sides **first**, saving the straight edge for **last**. (Fig. 9)

23) Repeat steps 21 and 22 for the other half. This will finish the lining for the pouch. (Fig. 10)

24) The diagram below shows the order in which the sides should be stitched together. Make sure the stitches are taut. A clip may be helpful to hold sections together while joining.

Half of the Zippered Pouch

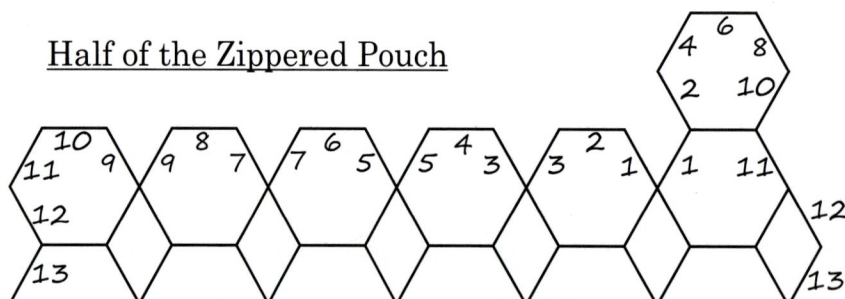

Round Zippered Pouches

25) Working from the right side, assemble the case. Join the shapes together with a closely spaced whip stitch through the top layer only. (Fig. 11)

26) After joining sides 1 and 2, travel the thread between the layers of fabric to the next starting point. Secure the thread with an extra stitch and repeat until all sides of the unit are joined. (Fig. 12)

27) Repeat steps 25 and 26 for the other half.

Open and close the zipper as necessary when joining the halves together.

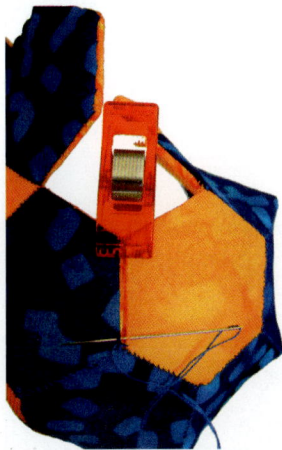

Fig. 11
Joining sides

Fig. 12
Travel the thread to the start of the next side.

Half of Zippered Pouch completed

Zippered Pouch completed

Sugar Tree Ornament

I named this ornament after a German tradition. At Christmas, the tree was decorated with so many candy-filled ornaments that the tree was referred to as the Sugar Tree.

Sugar Tree Ornament

Materials

3/4" Sugar Tree Ornament
Finished Size
1-1/2" x 1-3/4" x 4"

Paper Pieces Required
(6) 3/4" Hexagons (HEX075)
(3) 3/4" Half Hexagons (HHX075)
(6) 3/4" 6 Point Diamonds (6DIA075)
(3) 3/4" Equilateral Triangle (TRI075)

Fabric Required
Hexagons and Half Hexagons:
2" x 13"

Diamonds and Triangles:
1-1/4" x 13-1/2"

Lining:
4-3/4" x 5-1/2"

71F Pellon® Peltex® 1-Sided Fusible Ultra-Firm Stabilizer:
4-1/4" x 5"

Items Required
1/4" Wide Ribbon:
24"

Optional: Bell
3/8" Diameter

Making the Lining

Fig. 4

1) Baste all Paper Pieces according to the general English Paper Piecing instructions on page 3.

I used a small scale Christmas print for the hexagons and half hexagons.

2) Sew a half hexagon to the top of two hexagons. (Fig. 1)

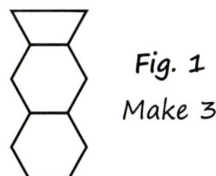

Fig. 1
Make 3

3) Sew a triangle to the bottom and two diamonds to the left side of the unit in Fig. 1. (Fig. 2)

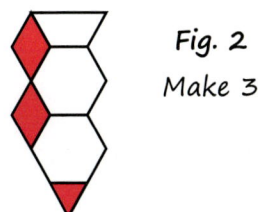

Fig. 2
Make 3

4) Sew all the units made in Fig. 2 together to make a row. (Fig. 3)

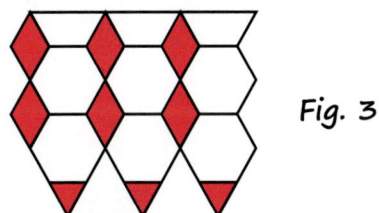

Fig. 3

5) Press the finished piece with the Paper Pieces still in place. Be sure that all the edges are as straight and even as possible.

6) Lay the finished piece face up over the non-shiny side of the fusible, and trace with a marking tool. (Fig. 4)

7) Cut the fusible 1/16" inside of the marked line.

8) Place the shiny side of the fusible down onto the wrong side of the lining fabric.

9) Following the manufacturer's directions, iron the fusible to the back of the lining fabric.

Sugar Tree Ornament

10) Trim the lining fabric, leaving approximately 1/4" seam allowance on all sides.

11) Clip the inside corners.

12) Fold the top straight edge of the lining over the fusible and press. (Fig. 5)

13) Fold the remaining seam allowances over the edges of the fusible, creating pleats at each corner, and baste in place with thread. (Fig. 6)

Fig. 5
Fold straight edge over and press.

Fig. 6
Clip the inside corners and baste the seams down with thread.

14) Remove all Paper Pieces from the finished top.

15) On the back of the fused lining, mark two lines 1-1/8" from both ends of the straight edge. (Fig. 7)

16) Cut two pieces of ribbon 12" long. Center and **glue baste** one end of each ribbon over the marked lines about 1/2" down from the straight edge. (Fig. 8)

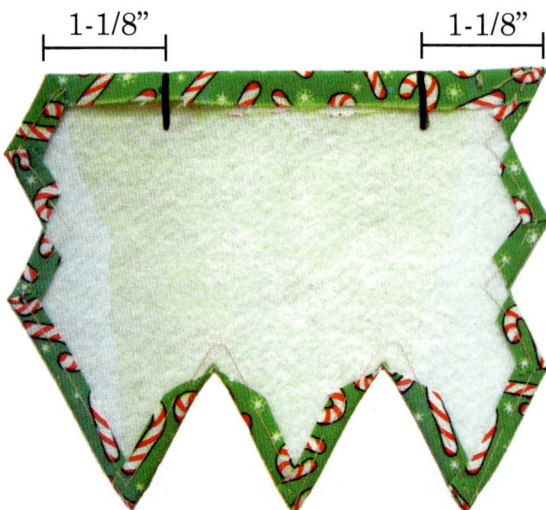

1-1/8"   1-1/8"

Fig. 7
Mark lines for ribbon placement.

Fig. 8
Ribbons glued in place

Sugar Tree Ornament

17) With the wrong sides together, join the finished piece to the lining using a combination of blind and whip stitches. Stitches will be less visible with the blind stitch, but a whip stitch with a shorter stitch length will be necessary for the inner corners where the seam allowance on the lining is very narrow. Be sure to secure the ribbon with extra stitches on either side.

18) The diagram below shows the order in which the sides should be stitched together. Make sure the stitches are taut. A clip may be helpful to hold sections together while joining.

Sugar Tree Ornament

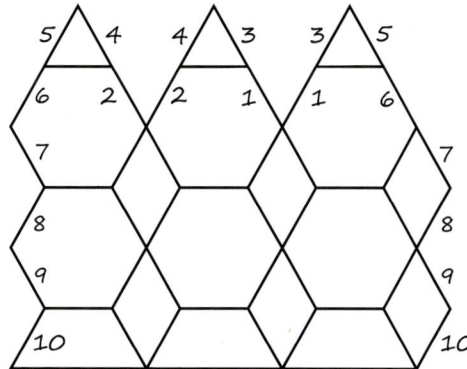

19) Working from the right side, assemble the ornament. Join the shapes together with a closely spaced whip stitch through the top layer only. (Fig. 9)

20) After joining side 1, travel the thread between the layers of fabric to side 2 and whip stitch together. For sides 3 to 5, you will want to change thread to match the color of the pieces. Change the thread again to finish joining the remaining sides.

If you see the lining showing through the seam on side 5, whip stitch over the seam a second time.

21) *Optional*: Attach the bell to the bottom.

22) Tie the ends of the ribbon into a bow.

Fig. 9
Stitching sides together

Finished Sugar Tree Ornament

Drawstring Bags

Do you need a bag for a gift? Do you want a bag to carry your tablet? You've found the right project!

Drawstring Bags

Materials

1" Octagon Bottom
Small Bag
Finished Size
6" x 6" x 10-1/2"

Paper Pieces Required
(16) 1" Hexagons (HEX100)
(8) 1" Half Hexagons (HHX100)
(16) 1" 6 Point Diamonds (6DIA100)
(1) 1" Octagon (OCT100)

Fabric Required
(8) Hexagons and (4) Half Hexagons:
2-1/2"x 24"

(8) Hexagons and (4) Half Hexagons:
2-1/2"x 24"

(16) Diamonds, Octagon, and Contrasting Band:
1/8 yard

Gathered Top:
19" x 15-1/2"

Pocket:
6-1/2" x 13-1/2"

Lining:
7-3/4" x 18"

987F Pellon® Fusible Fleece:
7" x 17-1/4"

Items Required
Grosgrain Ribbon or Cording:
2 yards

1-1/2" Octagon Bottom
Medium Bag
Finished Size
9" x 9" x 14"

Paper Pieces Required
(16) 1-1/2" Hexagons (HEX150)
(8) 1-1/2" Half Hexagons (HHX150)
(16) 1-1/2" 6 Point Diamonds (6DIA150)
(1) 1-1/2" Octagon (OCT150)

Fabric Required
(8) Hexagons and (4) Half Hexagons:
1/8 yard

(8) Hexagons and (4) Half Hexagons:
1/8 yard

(16) Diamonds, Octagon, and Contrasting Band:
5-1/4" x width of fabric

Gathered Top:
27" x 21-1/2"

Pocket:
8-1/2" x 20-1/2"

Lining:
11" x 26-1/2"

987F Pellon® Fusible Fleece:
10-1/2" x 26"

Items Required
Grosgrain Ribbon or Cording:
2-1/2 yards

2" Octagon Bottom
Large Bag
Finished Size
11" x 11" x 19"

Paper Pieces Required
(16) 2" Hexagons (HEX200)
(8) 2" Half Hexagons (HHX200)
(16) 2" 6 Point Diamonds (6DIA200)
(1) 2" Octagon (OCT200)

Fabric Required
(8) Hexagons and (4) Half Hexagons:
1/4 yard

(8) Hexagons and (4) Half Hexagons:
1/4 yard

(16) Diamonds, Octagon, and Contrasting Band:
1/4 yard

Gathered Top:
1 yard

Pocket:
9-1/2" x 28-1/2"

Lining:
1/2 yard

987F Pellon® Fusible Fleece:
1/2 yard

Items Required
Grosgrain Ribbon or Cording:
3 yards

Making The Pieced Bottom

1) Baste all Paper Pieces according to the general English Paper Piecing instructions on page 3.

2) Alternating colors, sew a half hexagon to the top of two hexagons. (Fig. 1)

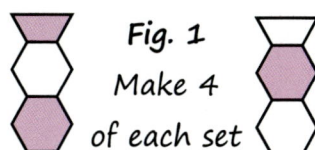

Fig. 1
Make 4
of each set

Drawstring Bags

3) Sew two diamonds to the left side of the units in Fig. 1. (Fig. 2)

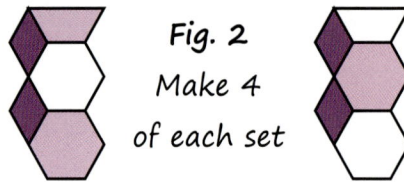

Fig. 2
Make 4
of each set

4) Alternating colors, sew all the units made in Fig. 2 together to make a row. Sew the octagon to the bottom of the first hexagon column. (Fig. 3)

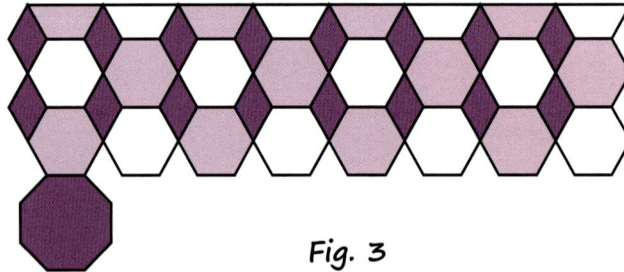

Fig. 3

Making the Lining

5) Press the finished piece with the Paper Pieces still in place. Ensure that the edges are as straight and even as possible.

6) Lay the finished piece face up over the non-shiny side of the fusible fleece and trace it with a marking tool.

7) Cut the fusible fleece 1/16" inside of the marked line. (Fig. 4)

8) Place the shiny side of the fusible down onto the wrong side of the lining fabric.

9) Following the manufacturer's directions, iron the fusible fleece to the back of the lining fabric.

10) Trim the lining fabric leaving approximately 1/4" seam allowance on all sides. (Fig. 5)

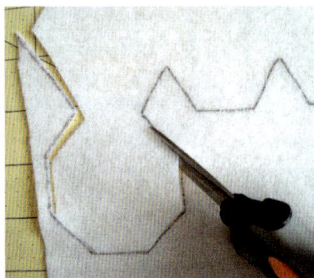

Fig. 4
Cutting the fusible fleece just inside
the traced line

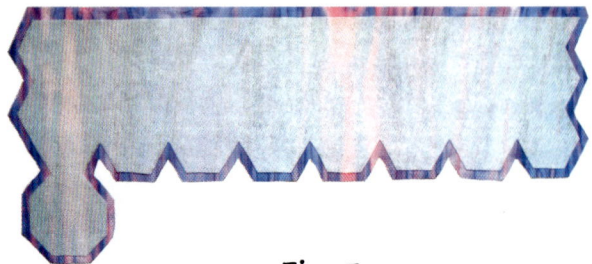

Fig. 5
Lining cut with 1/4" seam allowance
around the fusible fleece

Drawstring Bags

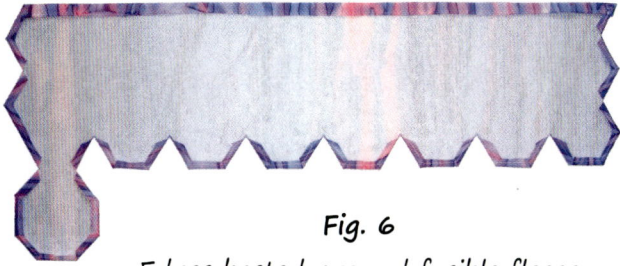

Fig. 6
Edges basted around fusible fleece

11) Fold the seam allowance over the straight edge of the fusible fleece and press.

12) Clip the inside corners. Fold the remaining seam allowances over the edges of the fusible fleece, creating pleats at the corners. Baste all sides in place with thread. (Fig. 6)

13) Remove all Paper Pieces.

14) With wrong sides together, join the finished piece to the lining (**except for the straight edge**) using a combination of blind and whip stitches. Stitches will be less visible with the blind stitch, but a whip stitch with a shorter stitch length will be necessary for the inner corners where the seam allowance on the lining is very narrow. Set pieced bottom aside.

Making the Gathered Top

Small Bag
Cut Fabric Required

Contrasting Band:
1-1/2" x 17-1/2"

Gathered Top:
(2) 9-1/4" x 15" pieces

Pocket:
6" x 13"

Cut Ribbon Required

Grosgrain Ribbon or Cording:
(2) 1 yard pieces

Medium Bag
Cut Fabric Required

Contrasting Band:
1-1/2" x 25-1/2"

Gathered Top:
(2) 13-1/4" x 21" pieces

Pocket:
8" x 20"

Cut Ribbon Required

Grosgrain Ribbon or Cording:
(2) 1-1/4 yard pieces

Large Bag
Cut Fabric Required

Contrasting Band:
1-1/2" x 33-1/2"

Gathered Top:
(2) 17-1/4" x 28" pieces

Pocket:
9" x 28"

Cut Ribbon Required

Grosgrain Ribbon or Cording:
(2) 1-1/2 yard pieces

15) Cut the two pieces of fabric required for the gathered top. If you are using a striped fabric, be sure to line up the stripes in the same direction.

Drawstring Bags

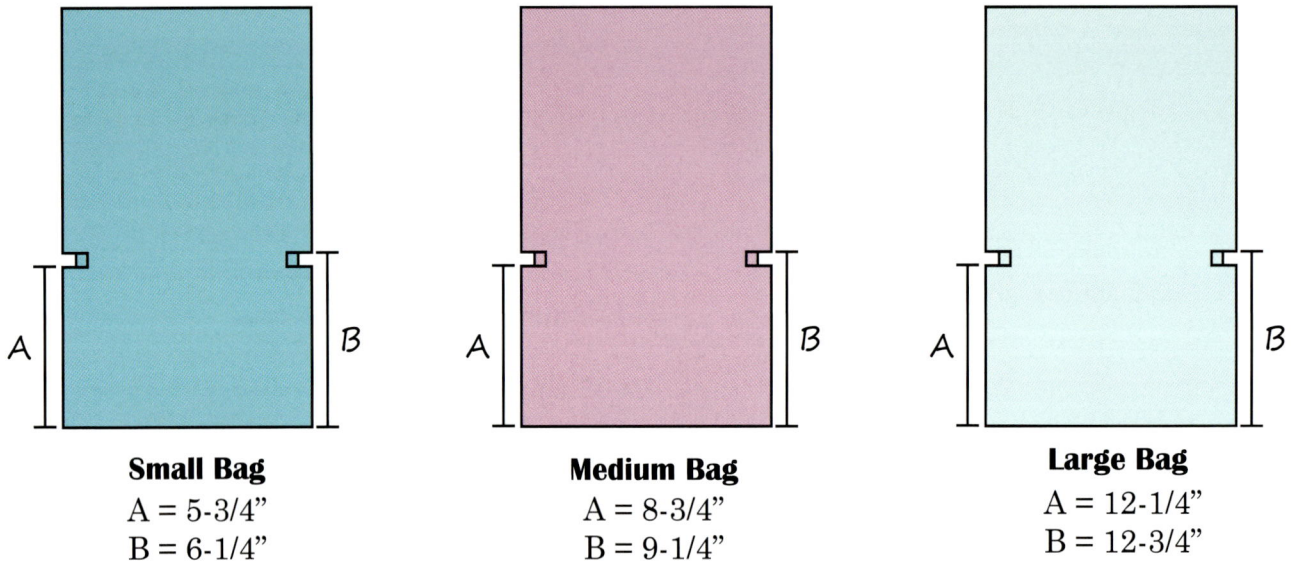

Small Bag
A = 5-3/4"
B = 6-1/4"

Medium Bag
A = 8-3/4"
B = 9-1/4"

Large Bag
A = 12-1/4"
B = 12-3/4"

16) Mark the openings for the drawstring on the pieces for the gathered top. On the wrong side of one of the gathered top pieces, mark points A and B by measuring from the bottom edge up. See diagrams above. Repeat for the other side.

17) Make a 1/2" cut into the fabric at points A and B to create a notch with a tab. Repeat for the other side. (Fig. 7)

18) Flip both of the fabric tabs to the wrong side of the fabric and fold under the 1/4" seam allowance. Press.

19) Sew the tabs down using a top stitch on the edge. (Fig. 8)

20) Repeat steps 16 through 19 for the other piece of the gathered top.

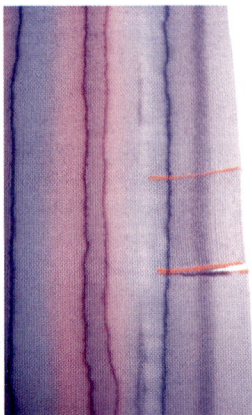

Fig. 7
Marked and notched

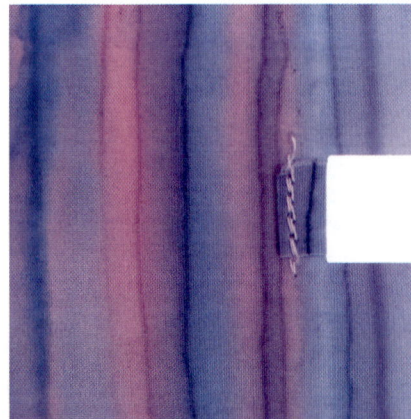

Fig. 8
Tab folded and top stitched in place

Drawstring Bags

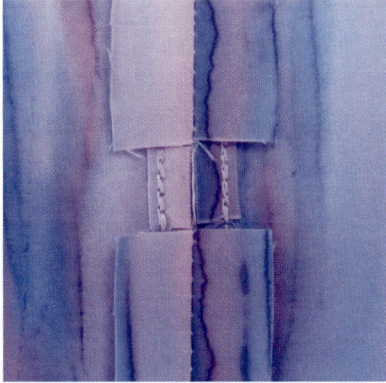

Fig. 9

Side seam stitched and
pressed open

Fig. 10

Contrasting band attached with
right side of fabric showing

21) With the right sides together, lay both pieces of the gathered top together matching the notches. Pin the pieces together.

22) Stitch only one side seam of the gathered top together using a **1/2" seam allowance.** Press the seam open. (Fig. 9)

23) With right sides together, pin the contrasting band to the bottom edge of the gathered top (the edge closest to the notches).

24) Stitch the contrasting band to the bottom edge using a **1/2" seam allowance**. Press the seam open. (Fig. 10)

25) With the right sides together, fold the top edge of the gathered top down to the bottom edge of the contrasting band. Pin the sides in place.

26) Stitch both side seams with a **1/2" seam allowance**. Be careful **not** to stitch the notches closed. (Fig. 11)

27) Clip the corners, turn right side out and press the raw edges even. (Fig. 12)

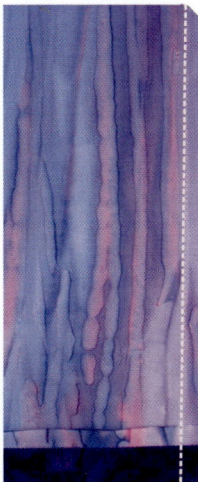

Fig. 11

Close up photo of side seam
stitched and corner clipped

Fig. 12

Right side out and pressed

Drawstring Bags

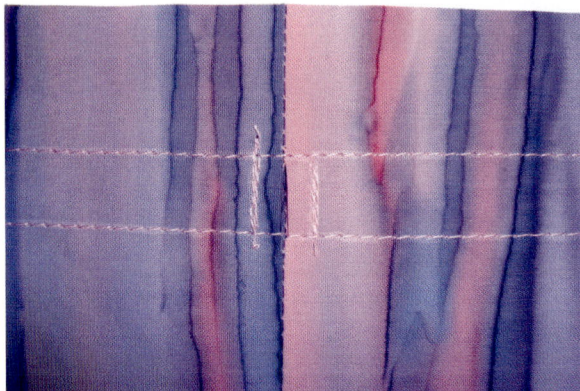

Fig. 13

Rod pocket for the drawstrings

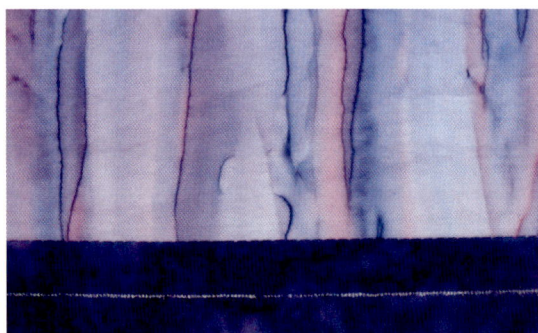

Fig. 14

Marked line on contrasting band

28) Create a rod pocket for the drawstrings by marking 1" and 1-1/2" from the folded edge of the gathered top. Following the marks made, stitch two parallel seams on the top. The drawstring openings should fall in the channel formed by the parallel seams. (Fig. 13)

29) Mark a straight line 1/2" up from the bottom edge on both sides. (Fig. 14)

30) Take the previously paper pieced bottom of the bag. Insert the gathered top into the opening on the straight edge of the bottom of the bag.

31) Use the marked lines as a guide to line up the straight edge of the body of the bag. Pin it in place through all layers. Pocket will be inserted here later. Set the gathered top aside.

Making the Pocket

32) With the right sides together, fold the pocket fabric in half, lining up the short sides of the rectangle.

33) Stitch both side seams using a **1/2" seam allowance**. Clip the corners (Fig. 15), turn right-side-out, and press.

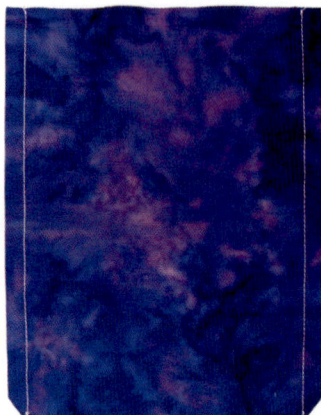

Fig. 15
Side seams sewn and
corners clipped

Drawstring Bags

Fig. 16

Side seams sewn

34) With the raw edge at the top and the folded edge at the bottom, fold the bottom edge of the pocket up again until it is 1/2" from the top raw edge. Press.

35) Top stitch both side seams of the pocket. This will form the pocket opening. (Fig. 16)

36) Flip the pocket to the back side and mark 1/2" from the raw edge with a ruler.

Attaching the Pocket

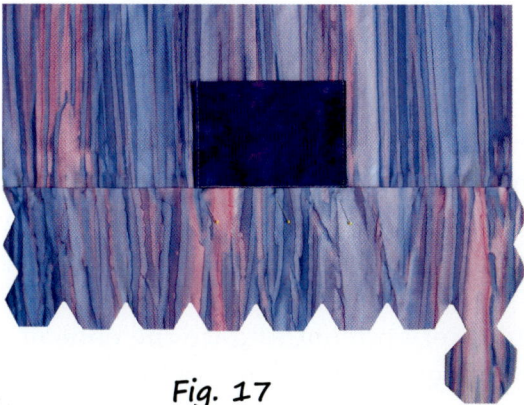

Fig. 17

Finished pocket pinned in place

Do not insert the pocket past the marked line or the opening of the pocket could be sewn shut.

37) With the wrong side of the pocket visible, place the pocket on top of the inner lining making sure the raw edges are down.

38) Insert the raw edges of the pocket into the lining of the main body of the bag. Remove pins as necessary.

39) Using the marked line on the back of the pocket as a guide, pin the pocket in place through all of the layers. (Fig. 17)

40) Flip the entire piece over to the right side. Top stitch the straight edge of the main body to the gathered top through all the layers.

41) Flip the entire piece over to the wrong side and press the pocket towards the bottom of the drawstring bag. Check to make sure that the opening of the pocket was not sewn shut.

Joining the Bottom of the Bag

Fig. 18

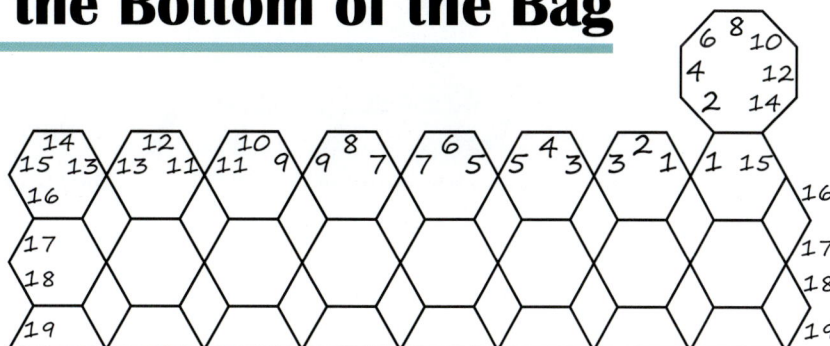

Drawstring Bags

Fig. 19

Be careful not to sew the drawstring openings shut.

42) Figure 18 on page 47 shows the order in which the sides should be stitched together. Make sure the stitches are taut. A clip may be helpful to hold the sections together while joining. (Fig. 18)

43) After joining sides 1 and 2, travel the thread between the layers of fabric to the next starting point. Secure the thread with an extra stitch and repeat until all sides of the unit are joined.

44) When the entire piece has been whip stitched together continue whip stitching the second side seam of the gathered top. Be careful not to sew the drawstring openings shut. (Fig. 19)

45) Make the drawstring. Take one end of a ribbon and pin a safety pin to it. Insert the pin through one of the drawstring openings. Follow the entire rod pocket and exit through the same opening. (Fig. 20)

46) Take the safety pin out and tie the ends of the ribbon together using a slip knot.

47) Repeat steps 45 and 46 using the drawstring opening on the opposite side of the bag. (Fig. 21)

Fig. 20
One drawstring ribbon inserted through drawstring opening

Fig. 21
Finished Drawstring Bag with ribbons inserted and tied in both drawstring openings.

Chatelaines

Never lose your scissors or thimble again! I like to have my tools ready at all times, so I created these chatelaines to wear around my neck while I'm making my projects. Now I always know where to find my scissors and thimble.

Small Chatelaine

Materials

1/2" Small Chatelaine
Finished Size
1" x 1" x 2"

Paper Pieces Required
(6) 1/2" Hexagons (HEX050)
(3) 1/2" 6 Point Diamonds (6DIA050)
(4) 1/2" Equilateral Triangle (TRI050)

Fabric Required
Hexagons:
1-1/2" x 9"

Diamonds and Triangles:
1" x 8-1/2"

Lining:
3" x 4"

71F Pellon® Peltex® 1-Sided
Fusible Ultra-Firm
Stabilizer:
2-1/2" x 3-1/2"

Items Required
Seed Beads:
27" Long Strand

Optional Embellishments:
(3 - 6) hot-fix flat back crystals
(6) crystal beads in various sizes

Making the Lining

Fig. 4

1) Baste all Paper Pieces according to the general English Paper Piecing instructions on page 3.

2) Sew a hexagon to the top of a hexagon. (Fig. 1)

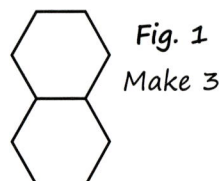

Fig. 1
Make 3

3) Sew a triangle and a diamond to the left side of the unit in Fig. 1. (Fig. 2)

Fig. 2
Make 3

4) Sew all the units made in Fig. 2 together to make a row. Sew the last triangle to the bottom of the first hexagon column. (Fig. 3)

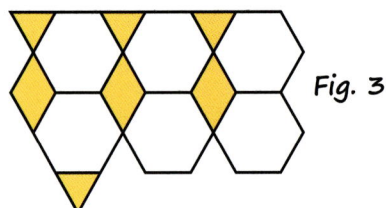

Fig. 3

5) Press the finished piece with the Paper Pieces still in place. Be sure that all the edges are as straight and even as possible.

6) Lay the finished piece face up over the non-shiny side of the fusible and trace with a marking tool.

7) Cut the fusible 1/16" inside of the marked line.

8) Lay the finished piece back over the fusible and flip the base triangle back. With a marking tool, draw a line on the fusible at the fold. Cut the fusible on the line. (Fig. 4)

Small Chatelaine

Fig. 5

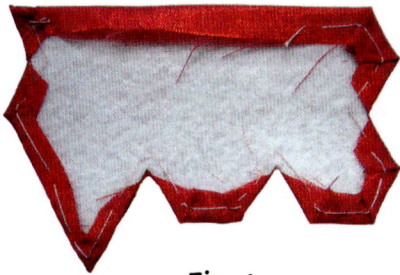

Fig. 6

Fig. 7

9) Place the shiny side of the fusible down onto the wrong side of the lining fabric. Make sure to place the cut off triangle back in its original position.

10) Following the manufacturer's directions, iron the fusible to the back of the lining fabric.

11) Trim the lining fabric leaving approximately 1/4" seam allowance on all sides. (Fig. 5)

12) Fold the seam allowance over the straight edge of the fusible and press.

13) Clip the inside corners. Fold the remaining seam allowances over the edge of the fusible, creating pleats at the corners. Baste all sides in place with thread. (Fig. 6)

14) Remove all Paper Pieces.

15) With the wrong sides together, join the finished piece to the lining using a combination of blind and whip stitches. Stitches will be less visible with the blind stitch, but a whip stitch with a shorter stitch length will be necessary for the inner corners where the seam allowance on the lining is very narrow.

16) *Optional:* If you are going to embellish your chatelaine with crystals or beads, now is the time to attach them. It is much easier to add them now, while the piece is flat, than it will be when the chatelaine is assembled. See embellishments section page 55 for more information. (Fig. 7)

17) Fold back the base triangle towards the lining and press it with an iron. If desired, attach the decorative beads to the bottom before assembling the chatelaine.

Small Chatelaine

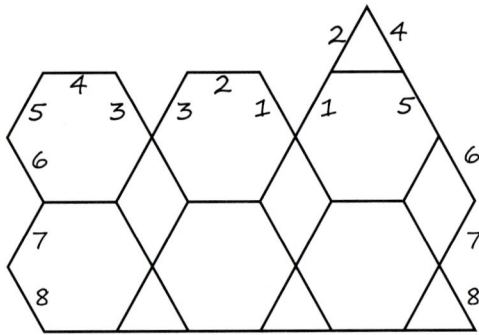

Fig. 8

18) The diagram shows the order in which the sides should be stitched together. Make sure the stitches are taut. A clip may be helpful to hold the sections together while joining. (Fig. 8)

19) Working from the right side, assemble the chatelaine. Join the shapes together with a closely spaced whip stitch through the top layer only. (Fig. 9)

20) After joining sides 1 and 2, travel the thread between the layers of fabric to the next starting point. Secure the thread with an extra stitch and repeat until all of the sides of the chatelaine are joined.

21) Secure a long strand of strong thread to the top edge of the chatelaine. String the seed beads to the desired length (approximately 27" long).

22) Stitch the remaining end to the opposite edge of the chatelaine.

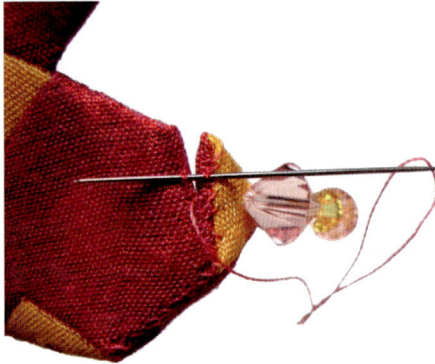

Fig. 9
Joining sides together

Finished Small Chatelaine

Large Chatelaine

Materials

1/2" Large Chatelaine
Finished Size
1" x 1" x 3-1/4"

Paper Pieces Required
(9) 1/2" Hexagons (HEX050)
(6) 1/2" 6 Point Diamonds (6DIA050)
(6) 1/2" Equilateral Triangle (TRI050)

Fabric Required
Hexagons:
1-1/2" x 13-1/2"

Diamonds and Triangles:
1" x 15"

Lining:
4" x 4"

71F Pellon® Peltex® 1-Sided
Fusible Ultra-Firm
Stabilizer:
3-1/2" x 3-1/4"

Items Required
Seed Beads:
27" Long Strand

Optional Embellishments:
(12) Hot-fix flat back crystals
(6) Crystal beads in various sizes

Making the Lining

Fig. 4

1) Baste all Paper Pieces according to the general English Paper Piecing instructions on page 3.

2) Sew 3 hexagons in a column. (Fig. 1)

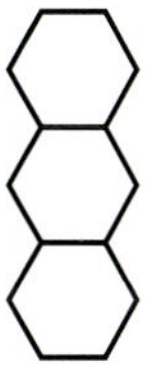

Fig. 1
Make 3

3) Sew a triangle and two diamonds to the left side of the unit in Fig. 1. (Fig. 2)

Fig. 2
Make 3

4) Sew all the units made in Fig. 2 together to make a row. Sew the last three triangles to the bottom of each unit. (Fig. 3)

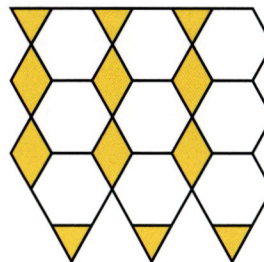

Fig. 3

5) Press the finished piece with the Paper Pieces still in place. Be sure that all the edges are as straight and even as possible.

6) Lay the finished piece face up over the non-shiny side of the fusible and trace with a marking tool.

7) Cut the fusible 1/16" inside of the marked line.

8) Place the shiny side of the fusible down onto the wrong side of the lining fabric.

9) Following the manufacturer's directions, iron the fusible to the back of the lining fabric.

10) Trim the lining fabric leaving approximately 1/4" seam allowance on all sides. (Fig. 4)

Large Chatelaine

Fig. 5

Fig. 6

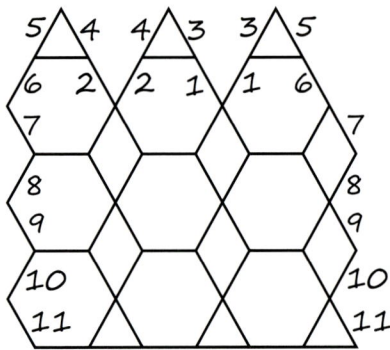

Fig. 7

Finished Large Chatelaine

11) Fold the top straight edge of the lining over the fusible and press.

12) Clip the inside corners. Fold the remaining seam allowances over the edges of the fusible creating pleats at each corner and baste in place with thread. (Fig. 5)

13) Remove all Paper Pieces from the finished top.

14) With the wrong sides together, join the finished piece to the lining using a combination of blind and whip stitches. Stitches will be less visible with the blind stitch, but a whip stitch with a shorter stitch length will be necessary for the inner corners where the seam allowance on the lining is very narrow.

15) *Optional:* If you are going to embellish your chatelaine with crystals or beads, now is the time to attach them. It is much easier to add them now, while the piece is flat, than it will be when the chatelaine is assembled. See the embellishments section on page 55 for more information. (Fig. 6)

16) The diagram in figure 7 shows the order in which the sides should be stitched together. Make sure the stitches are taut. A clip may be helpful to hold sections together while joining. (Fig. 7)

17) Working from the right side, assemble the chatelaine. Join the shapes together with a closely spaced whip stitch through the top layer only.

18) After joining side 1, travel the thread between the layers of fabric to side 2 and whip stitch together. For sides 3 to 5, you will want to change thread to match the color of the pieces. Change the thread again to finish joining the remaining sides.

19) *Optional:* Attach the decorative beads to the bottom.

20) Secure a long strand of strong thread to the top edge of the chatelaine. String the seed beads to the desired length (approximately 27" long).

21) Stitch the remaining end to the opposite edge of the chatelaine.

Embellishments

Hot Fix Flat Back Crystals

You may have seen flat back crystals on quilts or other items but were intimidated to try them. The projects in this book are a perfect opportunity to try a new technique on a small scale. The jewel box necklace and the chatelaines have been "blinged" with crystals and make beautiful accessories to wear around your neck.

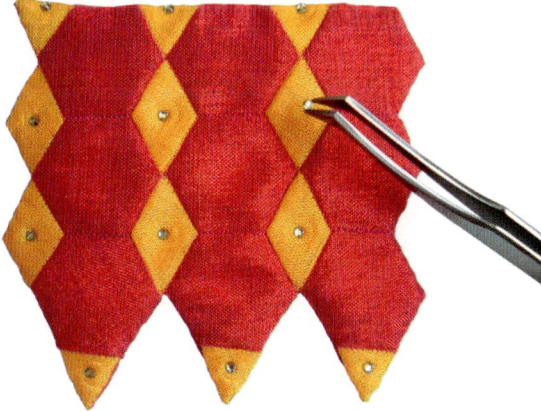

A pair of tweezers is necessary to pick up and place the tiny crystals onto your project. You will want to attach the crystals before your project has been assembled while it is still flat. Hot fix refers to the "glue" that is built into the back of the crystal. Different size crystals require a different length of time to heat the "glue" and adhere it to the fabric. Specialty irons can be purchased with blunt ends to make applying the crystals easier and at the correct temperature. Samples shown use size 6ss hot-fix, flat-back crystals, but the larger size 8ss could be used for even more sparkle. (Fig. 1)

Fig. 1

Placing crystals with tweezers

Beads and Bells

Beads can be used to hang the chatelaines or the sugar tree ornaments in place of the ribbon. They are not recommended to replace the chain for the jewel box necklace as the lid will not slide up and down as smoothly. If you are stringing beads to hang an item, make sure to use a strong thread like a beading thread.

Beads and/or bells are used as embellishments at the base of the chatelaines and sugar tree ornaments. They can also be used in place of the flat back crystals on any project. How about beads hanging from the diamonds on the drawstring bag? (Fig. 2)

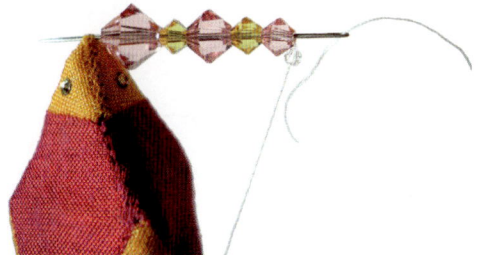

Fig. 2

Adding beads to chatelaines

Trims and Tassels

If desired, lace, trim, and embroidery can be added to the drawstring bag and the top edge of the jewel bowls, chatelaines, and sugar tree ornaments. Tassels are a great accent to the diamonds on the drawstring bag. Fancy tassels on the small drawstring bag made of shimmering fabric could be a great evening accessory. (Fig. 3)

Fig. 3

Tassels attached with seed beads

Resources

Material Resources

Paper Pieces ®
P.O. Box 68
Sycamore, IL 60178
1-800-337-1537 USA ONLY
1-815-899-0925 International
www.paperpieces.com

Perfect Circles ®
www.karenkaybuckley.com

PCP Group LLC (Pellon ®)
150 2nd Avenue North – Suite 1400
St. Petersburg, FL 33701
Toll Free: 800-223-5275

71F Pellon® Peltex® 1-Sided Fusible
Ultra-Firm Stabilizer

987F Pellon® Fusible Fleece

Clover Needlecraft, INC. ®
Clover Wonder Clips #3155
www.clover-usa.com

Connect with the Author

www.facebook.com/CSeesQuilts

www.CSeesQuilts.Etsy.com

CSeesQuilts@aol.com

http://www.youtube.com/watch?v=qLc3Apbr92E